Federal Furniture and Decorative Arts at Boscobel

FEDERAL FURNITURE and DECORATIVE ARTS at BOSCOBEL

Text by
Berry B. Tracy
with painting documentation by
Mary Black

Boscobel Restoration Inc. and
Harry N. Abrams, Inc. Publishers, New York

Designed by George Klauber and
Joseph Roberts, George Klauber Inc.

Library of Congress Cataloging in
Publication Data
Tracy, Berry B
    Federal furniture and decorative
    arts at Boscobel.
    Bibliography: p. 161
    Includes index.
    1. Furniture—New York (State)—
Garrison—History—19th century.
2. Decoration and ornament—Federal
style. 3. Art objects—New York (State)—
Garrison. 4. Garrison, N.Y. Boscobel.
5. Dyckman, States Morris—Homes—
New York (State). 6. Boscobel Restora-
tion, inc. I. Black, Mary C. II. Title.
    NK2406.T7
    749.2147′074′014732
    80-26062
ISBN 0-8109-0917-0
ISBN 0-8109-2246-0 (pbk.)

Library of Congress Catalog Card
Number: 80-26062

Published in Celebration of the
Twentieth Anniversary of the
Dedication of Boscobel: 1961–1981

Printed and bound in Japan

Contents

Preface

The genesis of this volume was the discovery, in 1975, of a faded copy of the inventory of States Dyckman's possessions, taken shortly after his death in 1806. The document raised many questions about the furnishings then on display in Boscobel, and initiated a period of extensive research and reevaluation.

It was the architectural beauty of Boscobel, rather than its historical associations, that guided its rescuers in the 1950's and encouraged the conception of Boscobel as States Dyckman's dreamhouse, recreating, on the banks of the Hudson, the elegance and luxury he had enjoyed during his extended sojourns in England. English and Continental furnishings were collected, and surviving examples of Dyckman's own purchases were overwhelmed by crystal chandeliers and elaborate floral carpets.

The discovery of the Dyckman inventory and the subsequent release to Boscobel of microfilms of the privately held Dyckman papers enabled us for the first time to document the construction and furnishing of Boscobel. The inventory began by listing quantities of window glass, shingles, dressed siding, lath, and other building materials, indicating that construction had barely begun at the time of Dyckman's death. This was confirmed by careful study of construction bills included in the Dyckman papers.

The inventory listed vast amounts of china, glass, and silver purchased by Dyckman in England, but little furniture, and the pieces that were listed were obviously of domestic manufacture. Further evidence was provided by a letter to States in London from his wife, approving his decision "not to bring furniture with you unless you think you can get a carpet for our parlour cheaper than in New York . . ." (Elizabeth Dyckman, New York, to "Dearest best beloved . . . ," January 15, 1802).

A picture emerged of States Dyckman's widow, Elizabeth, born and raised in northern Westchester County, but with family connections to New York merchant society, steadfastly completing the mansion according to her husband's plans, and then filling the spacious rooms with furniture ordered from New York cabinetmakers, furniture carefully selected to supplement the few pieces left to her by her husband. The Dyckman bills, for instance, confirm the purchase of twelve, light but strong, painted "bamboo" chairs to accompany the listed "dining table with ends Mahogany."

To redo a major historic house museum takes more than documentation. Mrs. Lila Acheson Wallace, co-founder with her husband of *The Reader's Digest*, had provided the funds necessary to reconstruct and furnish Boscobel initially, and had continued her generous support of its operation throughout the years. With courage and vision, she accepted the verdict implicit in the new findings and approved the major program of disposal and acquisition which followed. With her help, we were able, in two short years, to acquire the major collection of New York Federal furniture pictured within these pages.

This catalogue is respectfully dedicated to Mrs. Wallace, in everlasting gratitude for her steadfast devotion to Boscobel and to the principles of beauty and excellence that it represents.

Frederick W. Stanyer
Executive Director
Boscobel Restoration

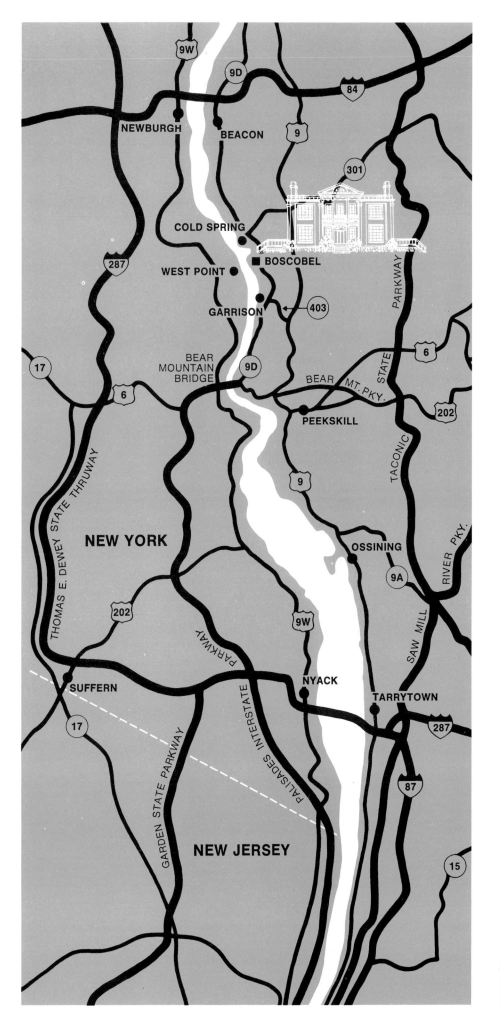

Map showing the present location of
Boscobel overlooking the Hudson River
and West Point.

The south facade of Boscobel as
reconstructed in Garrison-on-Hudson,
New York.

History of Boscobel

On May 21, 1807, the recently widowed Elizabeth Corne Dyckman sat down at her desk and penned an inquiry about her husband's estate to her London bankers. For the first time she headed her letter "Boscobell," her own casual misspelling of the name of her new home which was nearing completion on a bluff overlooking a broad expanse of the Hudson River about thirty-five miles north of New York City.[1]

Four years earlier, her husband, States Morris Dyckman, had ordered two snuff boxes made, incorporating in their lids medallions made of fragments of the legendary Royal Oak that had sheltered the beleaguered Charles II in the Forest of Boscobel in England.[2] One he presented to Elizabeth's Loyalist grandfather, the other to a good friend. And to the mansion that he dreamed of erecting beside the Hudson River he gave the name that symbolized his everlasting affection for England and its royal traditions.

Born in New York in 1755, States Dyckman descended from one of the early Dutch settlers of New Amsterdam. In 1776, as sentiment rose against the British royal prerogatives, he was employed as a clerk by the British Army's Quartermaster Department in New York.[3] His genteel manners and his skill with figures so impressed the Quartermaster General, Sir William Erskine, that Erskine, upon his retirement in 1779, took his young clerk with him to London. The accounts of Erskine's administration had to be prepared for approval by the government auditors, and, as the war dragged on and a British loss became a likelihood, the scrutiny became more intense—finally erupting in a full-scale investigation.

The point at issue was the profit realized by the successive Quartermaster Generals through their ownership of the wagons and horses which they rented to the army to transport men and materials during military campaigns. States skillfully served six defendants, including Erskine, and, according to the practice of the day, was rewarded with cash gifts and annuities. These provided him a substantial income.

Observing the taste and luxury of British society, States began to acquire tangible symbols of financial success: a fashionable wardrobe, silver and crystal, maps, prints, a telescope, and fifteen hundred elegantly bound books. Documents left by Dyckman reveal these purchases, and many of the surviving pieces are today displayed at Boscobel.

Elizabeth Corne Dyckman (1776–1823).

States Morris Dyckman (1755–1806).

Charles II before the great oak that sheltered him from his enemies in the Forest of Boscobel in England. The gold-and-enamel snuffbox (below) was made to order for States Dyckman. It bears a likeness of Charles II carved on a piece of the Royal Oak (left).

Meanwhile, using his brother as an agent, States purchased a farm for his mother near Peekskill, New York, and acquired other lands in the area totaling nearly one thousand acres.[4] With funds invested in stock in London and a promised annuity from Sir William Erskine, States Dyckman returned to New York in 1789 to "set down on my farm," knowing that time had healed the resentments caused by the differing loyalties during the Revolution. Several years earlier, a fellow Loyalist, Peter Van Schaack, had written him from America: "The distinction of Whig and Tory is no more."

States Dyckman proved to be a progressive farmer, using "Plaster of Paris" (lime) and crops such as vetch and clover to improve the soil. In 1794, his farm was described in glowing terms by the English agriculturist and traveler William Strickland: "A farm near Kings-ferry . . . in an high state of Cultivation, and improved as much as possible according to the ideas of the country and extremely well planted with the best kinds of fruit trees, now in high condition and full bearing, with a good house upon it...."[5]

All that States lacked was a wife. This he now found in the person of young Elizabeth Corne, granddaughter of his crusty Loyalist neighbor, Peter Corne. Corne had made his fortune as a sea captain and privateer, and increased it by marriage to Elizabeth Henderson, whose father was a Scotch-born physician and merchant with homes and store-

houses in New York City and sixteen thousand acres of land in the Mohawk Valley.[6]

Corne's oldest daughter, Letitia, married Dennis Kennedy, manager of the Corne grist mill near Peekskill. When the mill was confiscated by the Americans in 1777, Corne took the Kennedys' infant daughter, Elizabeth, to safety behind British lines on Long Island.[7] What became of Elizabeth's parents is not known, but thereafter young Elizabeth bore her grandfather's family name and was raised as his ward, returning with him to the Peekskill area after the war.

States and Elizabeth were married in Trinity Church in New York City on February 1, 1794. The groom was thirty-nine, the bride eighteen. Little is known of their courtship, but later letters reveal Elizabeth's adoration of her elegant and worldly husband. Prior to the marriage, States had remodeled his home and purchased new furniture and decorations from several fashionable New York establishments.[8] Funds for the acquisitions came, in part, from the sale of fourteen hundred books, purchased in London, to the noted Robert Livingston, Chancellor of New York State from 1777 to 1801.

Financial difficulties beset the couple almost immediately. The Erskine payments, irregularly received before the marriage, ceased entirely after Sir William's death in 1795 in spite of Dyckman's frequent appeals to Erskine's heirs. States was forced to sell the Kings Ferry farm

The fashionable Adelphi in London, as illustrated in *The Works in Architecture of Robert and James Adam, Esq.* Dyckman lived nearby from 1782 to 1788.

and to liquidate his London investments. In 1797, a few months after the birth of the Dyckmans' first child, named Peter Corne after Elizabeth's grandfather, States sold the wedding furniture.

Dyckman's pride prevented him from turning to Elizabeth's family for aid until 1799, when he offered to mortgage his remaining farm to Peter Corne in exchange for funds which would permit him to return to London to recover his fortune. The impending birth of the Dyckmans' second child—their daughter, Letitia—delayed States' departure until the spring of 1800, when he set sail, deep in debt to Corne and to Elizabeth's wealthy aunt, Margaret Corne Douglas.

Federal Hall and Wall Street in New York, with Trinity Church in the background, drawn by Archibald Robertson in 1798.

"Deep blue and white Jasper cameo," which States Dyckman purchased from Wedgwood & Byerley in 1803 and their London salesroom as it appeared in an 1809 edition of Rudolph Ackermann's *Repository of Arts, Literature, Commerce* . . . .

Soon after his arrival in London, States sent his wife elegant clothing and jewelry to belie any impression of impoverishment—scant comfort to Elizabeth, who, at twenty-four, had been left with responsibility not only for their two young children but also for the care of States' senile mother and the remaining farm. Soon the children fell ill with fever, which, as Elizabeth wrote her distant husband, "rages with such dreadful mortality in our whole neighborhood." The infant, Letitia, died in September 1800, followed two months later by old Mrs. Dyckman and then by the hired man.

Elizabeth ran the farm with increasing self-confidence, however, successfully nurturing a large shipment of fruit trees that States sent from England. In December 1801, she proudly wrote her husband that Chancellor Livingston had stopped by on his way to his assignment as Minister to France and had admired her nursery.

When States sailed for England, he had expected to complete his business with Erskine's heirs within a year. The matter dragged on, however, and he was called upon to assist General John Dalrymple, the last of the Quartermasters to have his records scrutinized. As States received payments from Dalrymple and the Quartermasters he had previously

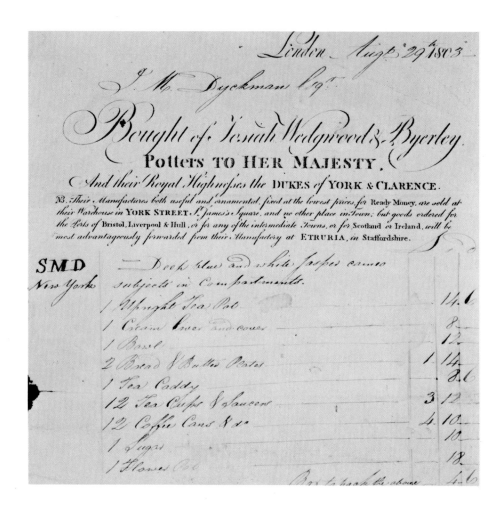

Bill from Wedgwood & Byerley to States Dyckman, dated August 29, 1803, listing his purchases of blue-and-white jasperware.

aided, he purchased books to replace those sold to Livingston and sent home a portfolio of prints, a spinning wheel, fabrics, gowns, cloaks, and other articles of current fashion.

At last, in 1802, the Erskine annuity was resumed and payments were made for the losses States had sustained as a result of his former employer's delinquency. This allowed States to repay his loan from Mrs. Douglas, and in the fall of 1803 he completed his work for General Dalrymple and received his final settlement. As he reported to Peter Corne:

> The benefits resulting from my long detention here . . . have been valued at about £8000 Stg or 36,000 Dollars[9] . . . I cannot therefore but flatter myself you will be satisfied and pleased to find that Extravagant as I have been since I came here, I have reserved something. . . .

Before sailing back to America, States indulged himself in one last shopping spree. On October 4, 1803, he wrote to Elizabeth:

> Yesterday I shipped on board the *Commerce* . . . 11 Trunks of Books and 20 Cases of Various articles as the Invoice sent to Mr. Lawrence [States' agent in New York] will explain. . . .

The invoice survives, as do many of the purchases, including part of a Wedgwood "Deep blue and white Jasper cameo" tea service, "A Rich Desert [sic] service painted in landscapes to order . . . ," a "Dessert Set richly cut" from John Blades, "Glass Manufacturer to His Majesty &

The Duke of York & Albany," who also provided a "Pair of 4 light Candelabras, Cut gilt & ornamented," purchased for £48 sterling.

After an absence of nearly four years, States Dyckman arrived in New York on January 1, 1804. In spite of persistent attacks of gout and the lingering effects of a leg injury sustained in a carriage accident, he began ordering materials for a new home that he had decided to build on his farm overlooking the Hudson River. In 1806, he wrote his London bankers: "Last year I began building a house in the country and unpromising as things look I must go on." No architectural drawings have been discovered, but a rough, unsigned sketch of a floor plan resembling Boscobel appears on the back of an 1804 grocery bill.

Construction began in earnest during the summer of 1806. The foundation was well under way in August when States Dyckman, weak-

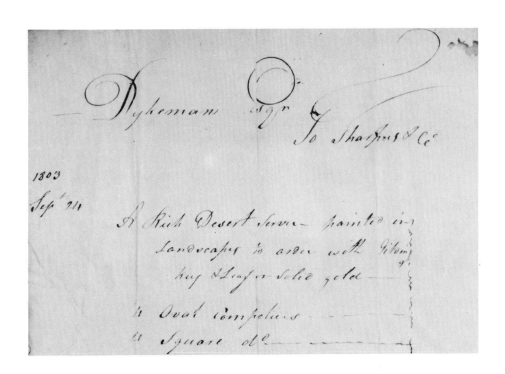

Examples of the Coalport porcelain "Rich Desert Service" purchased by Dyckman from Sharpus & Co. with the bill dated September 24, 1803.

An illustration of John Blades's showroom from Ackermann's *Repository* and examples of the cut glass purchased there by Dyckman in 1803.

ened by years of pain and ill health, died at the age of fifty-one. The inventory of his effects, dated September 1, 1806, shows that $1,537.50 worth of building materials had been stockpiled for the construction. Among the items listed were 382 panes of glass, 12" x 19"; 4,000 soft bricks; 10,000 shingles; and a large quantity of planks and boards.[10]

Little work was done on the house while Elizabeth Dyckman, now thirty years old, settled her husband's estate with the help of States' brothers and a family friend, Dr. John Kemp. Formal papers, naming Elizabeth administrator, along with Peter Corne and John Kemp, were filed on March 19, 1807.[11] Work was resumed on the house soon after.

States' cousin, William Vermilyea, worked as a carpenter and supervised the construction of Boscobel, but surviving correspondence indicates that Elizabeth participated actively in the project. The records are sketchy, but construction bills for work done through the spring of 1808 are among the Dyckman papers.

Elizabeth Dyckman's inheritance from her husband included more than 50 pounds of silver fashioned into elaborate tableware, tall gilt and crystal candelabras, 127 wine glasses, 3 mahogany dining tables, and quantities of china, cut glass, and silver plate. But the inventory was notably lacking in appropriate chairs for the new home. In 1807, Elizabeth bought 12 painted "Bamboo" Sheraton fancy chairs from William Palmer in New York, and a year later she ordered "12 Cross Back Green & Gold Fancy Chairs," with two matching settees, from Henry Dean, also of New York. It seems likely that the house was nearing completion by May 13, 1808, when Elizabeth ordered 37 yards of carpeting and "a carpet 5 x 6" from A. S. Norwood, the first carpet store in America.

The United States Census of 1820 confirms that Boscobel was then occupied by Elizabeth, her son Peter, and Peter's bride, Susan Matilda Whetton. The young Dyckmans' daughter, Eliza Letitia, was born two

years later. The house was staffed by five "free colored persons"—a significantly large number for the township. Curiously, although the property had earlier been considered a farm, none of the residents listed "agriculture" as their occupation.

Elizabeth Dyckman died in 1823, followed a year later by her son Peter. Shortly thereafter, Peter's widow, Susan Whetton Dyckman, married Edward Beverly Rathbone and bore him four children before his death in 1831. Thereafter, Susan married a third time, choosing Henry Cruger, heir to a neighboring estate. In 1838, title to Boscobel was transferred to sixteen-year-old Eliza Letitia, daughter of Susan and Peter Corne Dyckman, who had recently married her stepfather's youngest brother, John Peach Cruger.[12]

John Peach Cruger was described as a yachtsman and "country gentleman farmer."[13] He sought to produce income from the Boscobel lands by building and leasing several brick yards on the banks of the Hudson below the house.[14] However, before Cruger's death in 1888, title to Boscobel had passed to his creditors,[15] and from them to a succession

A sketch of a proposed floor plan for Boscobel, drawn on the back of an 1804 grocery bill found among the Dyckman papers.

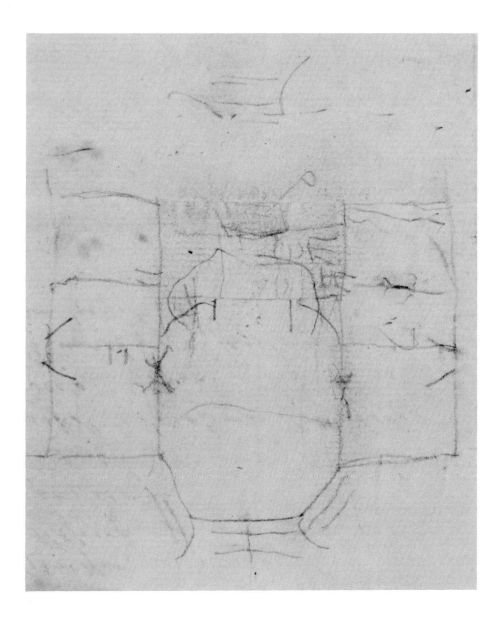

1915 photograph of the north facade of Boscobel on its original site in Montrose, New York. Opposite: architectural details being trucked onto Boscobel's new site in Garrison-on-Hudson.

of speculators until, in 1924, the premises were acquired by Westchester County for development as a park.

Last-minute efforts by interested citizens have twice saved Boscobel from destruction. In 1941, the Westchester County Park Commission threatened to demolish the building, but an organization was quickly formed to provide funds for maintenance and liability insurance. This organization, known as Boscobel, Inc., disbanded in 1947, assured that the Veterans Administration, which had purchased the property in 1945 as a location for a hospital, would utilize and preserve the mansion. But, by 1954, no use had been found for the building, and the General Services Administration declared Boscobel to be excess to the needs of the Veterans Administration, requiring removal from the site. Early in 1955, the GSA sold Boscobel to a demolition contractor for thirty-five dollars.

The story of the rescue is legend. Before a new organization could be formed to purchase Boscobel from the housewrecker, many of the architectural details were sold and removed to Long Island for incorporation in a new house being built there. In a last-ditch effort, funds were raised to purchase and dismantle the remaining portions of the house and to make copies to exchange for the originals on Long Island. Friends and supporters in Garrison, New York, emptied their barns to make room for the fragments of Boscobel. Forty-five acres of land were purchased in Garrison, which, like the original Dyckman farm, command a spectacular view of the Hudson River to the south and west. In the summer of 1957, ground was broken for the reconstruction of Boscobel in its new location.

Lila Acheson Wallace, who, with her husband, DeWitt Wallace, had founded *The Reader's Digest*, became an early supporter. Through her generosity, the mansion was rebuilt and furnished, and the grounds were landscaped. On May 21, 1961, the reconstructed home of States and Elizabeth Dyckman was formally opened. The Governor of New York State, Nelson A. Rockefeller, gave the principal address at the dedication ceremony, calling Boscobel "one of the most beautiful homes ever built in America."[16]

When, in 1975, research indicated that the furnishings were inconsistent with the newly discovered 1806 inventory of States Dyckman's estate, Mrs. Wallace funded a study which led to the disposal of the contents of Boscobel and the acquisition of the present collection of New York furniture of the Federal period. Today, the interiors are compatible with the many surviving Dyckman possessions and accurately reflect the taste prevailing during the years of Elizabeth Dyckman's occupancy.

Barbara W. Bielenberg
Assistant to the Executive Director
Boscobel Restoration

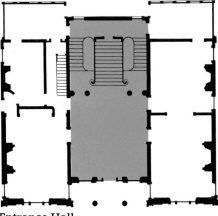

Entrance Hall.

The Collection

The building and furnishing of Boscobel from 1804 to 1820 coincided perfectly with the emergence of a new and cosmopolitan taste in America. Elizabeth Corne Dyckman's little city of New York had never before witnessed such rapid economic growth as it did in the first years of the nineteenth century. Perrin du Lac, the French author and local administrator, writing in 1801, found everything in the city in motion; "everywhere the shops resound with the noise of workers. . . . One sees vessels arriving from every part of the world, or ready to depart, and . . . one cannot better describe the opulence of this still new city than to compare it to ancient Tyre, which contemporary authors called the queen of commerce and the sovereign of the seas." Seven hundred new buildings appeared in the year 1804, and in 1805 William Johnson of Newton, New Jersey, looking for a business location, concluded that New York was "the London of America" and would undoubtedly "take the lead of business to any other place in the United States." From 1800 to 1810, the population increased by 36,000 to a total of 96,400, exceeding that of any other city in America.

Clearly, the society of this rapidly expanding economy needed quantities of fashionable furniture. In 1805–1806, the editors of the New York directory listed the city's cabinetmakers in a separate body for the first time. By way of introduction they remarked: "This curious and useful mechanical art is brought to a very great perfection in this city. The furniture daily offered for sale equals in point of elegance any ever imported from Europe and is scarce equalled in any other city in America."

Because of the extraordinary number of their labeled and documented pieces of exceptional quality that survive today, we know that Duncan Phyfe (working 1792–1847), Charles-Honoré Lannuier (working 1803–19), and Phyfe's neighbor, Michael Allison (working 1800–45), were by 1808 first among those whose work was thus praised. One of their many contemporaries in the trade, John Hewitt, noted in his ledger, in 1811, the comparative measurements of Phyfe's and Lannuier's wood columns, indicating that these two cabinetmakers were the leading executors of the new Classical style. Phyfe's work was exemplary of the Anglo-American Sheraton versions of the new New York style which predominates in the collections of furniture at Boscobel. Allison's many labeled pieces of furniture which have survived indicate that he followed very closely the quality of workmanship and taste of the leader, Phyfe.

It is evident from a watercolor drawing of Phyfe's workshop and warehouses on Fulton Street, executed about 1816 by John Reuben Smith, that his establishment was larger than those of his two major contemporaries, Allison and Lannuier. Phyfe seemingly enjoyed great success, for in 1816 Sarah Huger of New York wrote to relatives in Charleston of her difficulties in getting furniture executed for them by the busy Phyfe, stating that "Mr. Phyfe is so much the United States rage it is difficult to get an audience with him."

Patterns for New York mahogany furniture like that in the Boscobel collection were described and illustrated by the committees of master and journeyman cabinetmakers in the New York Cabinetmakers' Price Books of 1796, 1802, 1810, and 1817.

Their designs evolved with the changing fashion and economic growth, necessitating many new editions describing and pricing their wares. These guides established fair wages paid to the journeymen by the masters and they survive today, with their detailed listings of design elements and the cost of each, as records of the rapidly changing fashion.

The styles of furniture clearly emanated from English Sheraton and Regency, and French Directoire, Consulat, and Empire tastes. Perhaps the cabinetmakers' most important sources of designs were the books of George Hepplewhite, Thomas Shearer, Thomas Sheraton, Thomas Hope, and George Smith.

Duncan Phyfe's Workshop and Warehouses. Watercolor drawing, attributed to John Reuben Smith, c. 1816.

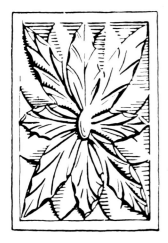

THE

NEW-YORK

REVISED PRICES

FOR

MANUFACTURING

CABINET AND CHAIR WORK.

—

June, 1810.

NEW-YORK:

PRINTED BY SOUTHWICK AND PELSUE,

No. 3, New-street.

....

1810.

New York carved rosette tablet and
the New York Price Book of 1810.

Second in importance were the design plates in the London price
books and fashion periodicals, Rudolph Ackermann's *Repository of Arts*
and Pierre la Mésangère's *Furniture and Objects of Taste* plus the oc-
casional importation of furniture by statesmen and merchants.

Few of the leaders in the development of New York's interpre-
tation of the Classical styles had European training except for the
celebrated emigré Lannuier, who was trained in Paris, presumably by
his accomplished older brother, Nicholas. Lannuier came to New York
in 1803 and made furniture in all the styles of Paris until he died in 1819.
He also made his own versions of Phyfe's furniture in the New York
Anglo-American Sheraton and Regency tastes and most certainly had
a profound influence on the formulation of all the New York furniture
styles of his time. Much of the elegant, reeded and carved mahogany
furniture of Sheraton derivation has the flowing curves and attenuated

architectural character of the French furniture of the periods of Louis XVI, the Consulat, and Directoire. By 1810, the Cabinetmaker's Price Book listed the details for making a "French bedstead," a "French sideboard," and a "French Press" or wardrobe, of which there are two in the Boscobel collection. The French wardrobes featured full-length doors from top to bottom allowing full visibility of sliding trays, shelves, and in some cases space for hanging dressing gowns and coats, distinguishing them from the English models, which were made in two parts with a lower case of drawers and an upper case with shelves or trays.

Other major developments in furniture forms at the turn of the nineteenth century reflected the current interest in luxury, comfort, convenience, and mobility. Sideboards with cupboards, drawers, and cellarette compartments superseded the colonial side table in dining rooms. Dining tables in sections of two to three parts with extra leaves, which could easily be moved for sweeping, and reduced or increased in size, superseded the single massive gateleg table of earlier forms.

The new mobility of Federal period furniture was achieved by the use of casters or rollers, particularly on sofas and tables of all descriptions. In the third quarter of the eighteenth century, rollers were sometimes used in a concealed fashion on Chippendale furniture. By the end of the century, they had become a visible and integral part of the design of the furniture, so much so that when removed by wear and later generations of owners, the successful scale of the furniture is impaired.

The earliest group of high-style furniture in the Boscobel collection relates to the dominant taste of the Hepplewhite (1788) and early Sheraton (1793-94) styles as interpreted in New York from the 1790's until about 1810. It is characterized by square, tapered legs, shield-shaped chair backs, delicate, contrasting light wood stringing and inlays, and the French feet and double swept apron typical of the bureaus labeled by Michael Allison. Most of the furniture, however, dates closely to the fashionable furnishing of the new mansion from 1808 to about 1820.

This larger group is predominantly of the late Sheraton (1803-12) and Regency (1811–20) influence characterized by turned and reeded legs, terminating in the favored New York foot of vasiform shape, "pillar and claw" pedestals, curule supports, and scroll-back chairs and

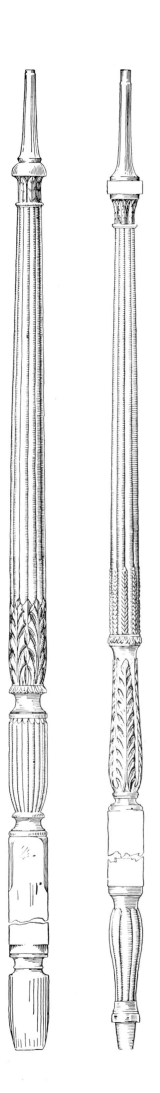

sofas. Fluting, reeding, and richly figured mahogany veneers, with cross-banded borders and carved tablets, are the principal ornament of this essentially geometric and architectural style of furniture, created by Duncan Phyfe and his contemporaries.

The principal exterior wood was West Indian mahogany of the finest quality. Occasionally, West Indian satinwood was used for desk interiors and sometimes for a whole piece. The secondary woods were mostly native ash, cherry, maple, white pine, and yellow poplar. A great part of the success of this furniture was in the rich color of the mahogany and its contrasting gilt-brass hardware. In the catalogue that follows, the furniture has been photographed in its restored state to illustrate clearly its original condition as it came from the workshops of New York in the first decades of the nineteenth century.

The furniture is presented in seven groups, related in form and function, and beginning with an introduction to each group. An eighth section illustrates the looking glasses, clocks, and chandeliers, and sections nine and ten illustrate respectively the small decorative arts and original Dyckman objects, and the paintings in the collection.

Berry B. Tracy
Curator-in-Charge of American Decorative Arts
The American Wing
The Metropolitan Museum of Art

From left to right: a lyre splat, a New York dining table, typical New York vasiform feet, New York high-bed posts, a pillar-and-claw support, and pedestals of "pillars."

Sofas, Settees, Chairs, Stools, and Benches

The most imposing forms of seating furniture of Federal New York are the elegant sofas of which Boscobel has three fine examples. The earliest of these is a "square-back" (1) with a central, rectangular, carved tablet that projects above the back frame or crest rail. It is a type commonly attributed to the cabinetmakers Slover and Taylor, but it was a standard in the Price Book of 1802, and could have been made in any one of the better shops. A slightly later development is the classic "scroll-back" sofa (4) with a carved crest rail of three tablets and with straight arms.

The richest, and latest, of the three models is a "Grecian Cross Front" sofa (10) with scrolled arms, en suite with twelve chairs (11) and a pair of stools (12). The curule-formed legs were drawn from detail plates in the London Price Book of 1808, and they became standard in New York in the seven years after the printing of the New York Price Book of 1810.

This particular suite is nearly identical to one in the Metropolitan Museum which, according to family tradition, was made for the New York merchant Thomas Cornell Pearsall in Duncan Phyfe's shop. The Boscobel suite was, by family tradition, made by Phyfe for the New York merchant Nathaniel Prime. Although both sets of chairs have cane seats, the Boscobel chairs differ in having rigid seats upholstered over removable wood frames rather than loose cushions. Both suites have the superb quality of form, construction, carving, and reeding that is identified with Phyfe's most important work.

Among the rarities in upholstered seating furniture at Boscobel are the "cabriole" chairs of which there is an early pair (3) from the Livingston family and a single example (17) with a reeded mahogany frame and paw feet, said to have been made by Duncan Phyfe for John Brevoort in 1817. It is an anglicized version of the "fauteuil gandole" of the Directoire and Empire styles. These Classical forms with low backs are a diversion from the standard high-back Hepplewhite wing or "easy chair" (2), which was frequently fitted with a chamber pot frame under a loose seat cushion and confined to use in bedchambers.

The earliest of the mahogany open arm chairs at Boscobel is a late eighteenth-century square-back (14) with five plain splats and scrolled arms in the Chippendale manner. It is believed to have belonged to Mrs. Dyckman's grandfather, Peter Corne, and is a sturdy form that was favored by conservative Hudson Valley and Long Island families.

Sets of chairs of all descriptions comprised a large part of the inventory of all prosperous homes in the Federal period. At Boscobel, the earliest of these sets are the shield-backs (6), which were called in the 1796 Price Book a "vase-back stay rail chair" with "serpentine top." They have a distinctive scalelike carving on the splats and as a type they are frequently found in Hudson Valley homesteads. Similar chairs, from the Glen Sanders house in Scotia, New York, are believed to have been made by Robert Carter of New York, and a pair at George Washington's house Mount Vernon are believed to be by Thomas Burling of New York.

An original Dyckman arm chair (8) with a scroll-back and cross splat, made between 1807 and 1810, is typical of Phyfe's early chairs and those made by his contemporaries. It relates to the set (7) with fluted top rails, which corresponds with the fluted and drapery-carved "scroll-back" sofa (4) and the pair of chairs (5) with carved drapery panels. The Dyckman arm chair (8) and a pair (9) descended in the Henderson family have concentric, horizontal reeding in the crest rails and are like the earlier shield-backs, a characteristic type frequently found in Hudson Valley families. The Phyfe sabreleg chair, with a lyre splat (16) of a little later fashion, is one from a large set made between 1815 and 1820, most of which is still owned by descendants of the Henderson family. Identical sets of this model of Phyfe's lyre-back chairs are in the Metropolitan Museum and the Henry Ford Museum.

The "lolling" or "Campeachy" chair, sometimes called a "Spanish" chair (15), was a comfortable

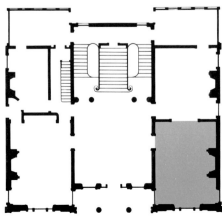

Front Drawing Room.

form, of Hispanic origin, favored in New Orleans and admired by Thomas Jefferson, who owned a similar chair by 1819. The form was known in New York before 1820. A splendid reeded example of great sophistication, worked in the manner of Duncan Phyfe, is found in the Winterthur Museum collection. Its curule legs are an adaption of the "Grecian stool" (12). The flat, scrolled arms with cabriole supports on Boscobel's Hudson Valley chair are like those on the Hispanic models.

By 1805, painted chairs and settees of Sheraton derivation had superseded the common windsors (24) in popularity and production. They were admired not only for their beauty, lightness, and strength, but because they were much cheaper than mahogany chairs. They were later sometimes made of "curled maple" (22), but usually highly ornamented by skilled hands on either red, black, bright green, or straw-colored ground, and had cane or rush seats. Mrs. Dyckman apparently favored the fancy furniture in the initial period of furnishing her new

home, for a bill of 1807 from William Palmer in New York indicates that she bought 12 "Bamboo" fancy chairs (18) and, in 1808, a bill from Henry Dean shows she purchased "12 Cross Back Green & Gold Fancy Chairs" with "2 Settees to Match" (19, 20). The making of fancy, painted furniture was a separate trade from that of working in mahogany. The tradition of painted decoration continued in handwork of a different character in the 1820's as seen in the Livingston family benches (21) and the later Dyckman-Cruger chairs (23).

The "Common" chair of all households in the Hudson Valley was, for over a hundred years, the yoke-back rush-bottom chair with pad feet and a broad, shapely back splat (25). Usually painted black, the chairs with their economy, ruggedness, and comfort caused this early eighteenth-century Dutch form to be made and advertised for sale in the *Albany Gazette* as late as 1810.

Two curule chairs by Duncan Phyfe are arranged near a square-back sofa attributed to Slover & Taylor of New York.

All dimensions are given in inches first, then in centimeters. H. stands for height, W. for width, D. for depth, L. for length, Diam. for diameter.

1 Sofa (square-back).
1800–1805, New York, attributed to Slover and Taylor.
H.40½ (102.9) L.80¼ (203.8) D.25 (63.5)
Mahogany, cherry, tulip poplar; yellow moreen upholstery.
Purchase, 1960.

1

1a Detail of crest-rail tablet (drapery-carved).

1a

2

2 Easy chair.
1795–1800, Pennsylvania or Maryland.
H.47(119.4) W.35(88.9) D.29(73.7)
Cherry, tulip poplar glue blocks, pine
frame; blue moreen upholstery.
Originally contained a chamber pot
board, which has been removed.
Purchase, 1960.

3 Cabriole chairs (pair).
1795–1805, New York or England.
H.39 (99.1) W.29½ (74.9) D.27 (68.6)
Mahogany, beech, pine blocks; yellow
moreen upholstery.
Purchased from Callendar House sale;
according to the Livingston family history, having come from Clermont, the
seat of Chancellor Robert Livingston.
Purchase, 1976.

4 Sofa (scroll-back, with 1 drapery-
carved, 2 fluted tablets on crest rail).
c. 1811, New York, attributed to Duncan
Phyfe's workshop.
H.37 (94.0) L.78 (198.1) D.33 (83.8)
Mahogany, tulip poplar, ash, pine; red
haircloth upholstery.
Purchase, 1977.

4

5

5a

5 Side chairs, 4 (scroll-back, cross-back with drapery panel).
1805–1810, New York.
H.33 (83.8) W.19⅛ (48.6) D.17¼ (43.8)
Mahogany, tulip poplar; red haircloth upholstery.
Gift of Rufus K. Dryer II, 1978.

5a Detail of side chair.

6 Chairs, 1 arm, 9 side (vase-back stay rail with serpentine top, fish-scale carving).
1795–1800, New York.
Arm: H.38(96.5) W.26(66) D.19(48.3)
Side: H.38(96.5) W.23(58.4) D.19(48.3)
Mahogany, maple; chestnut-brown hair-cloth upholstery with brass nails.
Purchase, 1962.

7

7 Chairs, 1 arm, 6 side (scroll-back, cross-back with fluted tablets on crest rail).
1805–1810, New York, attributed to Duncan Phyfe's workshop.
H.32½ (82.6) W.19½ (49.5) D.17 (43.2)
Arm chair measures same as side chair.
Mahogany, tulip poplar, pine; red hair-cloth upholstery.
Purchase, 1976.

9 Chairs (pair, with concentric, reeded
tablets on crest rails).
1805–1810, New York.
H.31⅞ (81.0) W.18⅞ (47.9)
D.16⅜ (41.6)
Mahogany, tulip poplar braces; cane
seats with blue moreen cushions,
not shown.
Descended in the Henderson family.
Purchase, 1962.

8 Arm chair (scroll-back, cross-back with
concentric, reeded tablet on crest rail).
1807–1810, New York.
H.33¼ (84.5) W.20⅝ (52.4)
D.17½ (44.5)
Mahogany, maple braces, pine blocks;
red haircloth upholstery.
Purchase, 1962.

10a

10 "Grecian" sofa (curule, scroll-back
with 2 carved tablets of cornucopia and
1 with seaweed and ribbon).
1810–1820, New York, Duncan Phyfe.
H.32½ (82.6) L.85¼ (216.5)
D.24½ (62.2)
Mahogany, four tulip poplar medial
"rocker" stretchers; yellow moreen up-
holstery.
Made for the New York merchant
Nathaniel Prime.
Purchase, 1970.

10a Detail of carved crest rail.

Rear Drawing Room.

11 Curule chairs, 12 (scroll-back with carved seaweed tablets on crest rail).
1810–1820, New York, Duncan Phyfe.
H.32¾ (83.2) W.17¾ (45.1)
D.16¼ (41.3)
Mahogany, tulip poplar medial stretchers; yellow moreen upholstery.
Made for the New York merchant Nathaniel Prime.
Purchase (4), 1970 (8), 1976.

12 Curule stools (pair).
1810–1820, New York, attributed to Duncan Phyfe's workshop.
H.18 (45.7) W.20½ (52.1) D.15¾ (40.0)
Mahogany, tulip poplar, ash rails; yellow moreen upholstery.
Made for the New York merchant Nathaniel Prime.
Purchase, 1976.

13 Footstools (pair, Ottoman-type).
1815–1820, New York.
H.8 (20.3) W.15 (38.1) D.15 (38.1)
Mahogany, pine; gilt-brass feet; yellow moreen upholstery.
Purchase, 1976.

11

13

12

14 Arm chair (square-back).
1780–1800, New York.
H.38 (96.5) W.30½ (77.5) D.23 (58.4)
Mahogany, original pine corner blocks
and cherry seat frame; old brown
leather upholstery.
Belonged to Peter Corne.
Purchase, 1962.

15 Lolling, Campeachy, or "Spanish" chair.
1816–1820, Hudson Valley, New York.
H.37 (94.0) W.29 (73.7) D.30 (76.2)
Mahogany throughout; brown leather
upholstery.
Gift of Berry B. Tracy, 1978.

14

15

16

16 "Grecian" chair (scroll-back, with lyre splat).
1815–1820, New York, attributed to Duncan Phyfe's workshop.
H.33 (83.8) W.19 (48.3) D.18 (45.7)
Mahogany, ash, tulip poplar, ebony; brass; black haircloth upholstery.
Descended in the Henderson family.
Gift of Berry B. Tracy, 1978.

17 "Grecian" chair (tub, cabriole).
c. 1817, New York, Duncan Phyfe.
H.32 (81.3) W.24 (61.0) D.24 (61.0)
Mahogany throughout, pine corner blocks; black haircloth upholstery.
Descended in the Brevoort family through the late Mrs. John Kane of Tuxedo, New York.
Purchase, 1976.

17a Detail of chair.

17

43

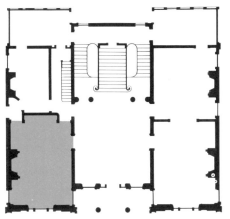

Dining Room.

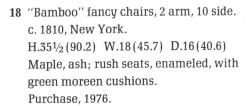

18 "Bamboo" fancy chairs, 2 arm, 10 side.
c. 1810, New York.
H.35½ (90.2) W.18 (45.7) D.16 (40.6)
Maple, ash; rush seats, enameled, with
green moreen cushions.
Purchase, 1976.

18

19 Chairs (fancy), 2 arm, 10 side.
1808, New York, Henry Dean.
Arm: H.32½ (82.6) W.20 (50.8)
D.16¼ (41.3)
Side: H.32½ (82.6) W.19 (48.3)
D.16¼ (41.3)
Maple, ash, whitewood, painted green,
brown, and gold; rush seat, enameled.
Five of the six originals are believed to
be from the set of "12 green and gold
crossbacks and 2 settees to match"
which Mrs. Dyckman purchased from
Henry Dean, gilder and fancy chair-
maker of New York, on January 15, 1808 .
Purchase (6), 1976; reproduction (6),
1976–1977.

20 Settee (fancy).
Reproduction, 1976, after a New York
"cross-back" settee of 1808–1810;
original is in the Abigail Adams Smith
Museum, New York City.
H.32½ (82.6) L.72½ (184.2)
D.20¾ (52.7)
Maple, ash, whitewood, painted green,
brown, and gold; rush seat, enameled.
Reproduction, 1976.

21 Benches, pair of "Grecian" (fancy).
    1815–1820, New York.
    H.33¾ (85.7) L.53½ (135.9) D.16 (40.6)
    Maple, cane, fois bois rosewood with
    gilt striping and freehand decoration of
    American eagles; cane seats.
    From Callendar House, Livingston
    family.
    Purchase, 1976.

22 Chairs (fancy), 4.
    1810–1820, New York.
    H.33 (83.8) W.18 (45.7) D.16 (40.6)
    Curled maple, ash; rush seats.
    Purchase, 1976.

47

23

24

24 Windsor chairs (pair with arms).
1790–1800, Connecticut or New York.
H.38(96.5) W.25(63.5) D.18(45.7)
Maple, ash, tulip poplar, painted green.
Purchase, 1962.

25 Chairs, Hudson Valley yoke-back, 8.
1760–1820, Hudson Valley, New York.
H.40½(102.9) W.20¼(51.4) D.16(40.6)
Maple, ash, tulip poplar, painted black;
rush seats, enameled.
Purchase, 1977.

25

49

Card Tables, Worktables, and Pembrokes

The card tables of Federal America were invariably made in pairs since their primary function was as ornament in the symmetrical room arrangements of the Classical era. Only secondarily were they used for the popular card games of the time, loo and whist. One rarely sees these tables surviving together from the early nineteenth century, yet the Boscobel collection boasts three handsome pairs made in New York between 1805 and 1820.

The earliest of these (26) is a "treble elliptical" pair with turned and reeded legs terminating in the favorite New York vasiform foot and fitted with gilt-brass ferrules (ball and collar). The ferrules are frequently found on New York Sheraton legs and are analogous to, if not derivative of, the similar French "toupie" or brass-bound feet used on French Consulat and Directoire table legs. Typical of New York card tables since the mid-eighteenth century is the fifth leg (rear left). Referred to by the cabinetmakers as a "fly leg," it opened on a gate to support the hinged top leaf. This five-legged pair of tables

is nearly identical in proportions and detail to two others labeled by the New York cabinetmaker John Dolan.

Quite different in character are the "pillar and claw" card tables (28) with blocky, ebonized paw feet. This form with three legs, two of which swing backward on internal iron rods when the leaf brackets are opened, was called a "Mechanical" card table and is today usually referred to as a "trick leg" table.

The D-shaped pair of card tables (27) with composite lyre-and-flame finial pedestals have all the extraordinary qualities of Phyfe modeling and construction. The base of the pedestal is finished with a raised or beveled panel, a favorite device of the Phyfe workshop between 1815 and 1820. The character of the carving on the lyres and particularly on the finials is like that on the pedestal of the Van Rensselaer "pillar and claw" tea table (44) made in Phyfe's shop about 1817. Similar card tables, attributed to Phyfe, are in the collections of the Albany Institute of History and Art and the Taft Museum.

The New York cabinetmakers'

price books spelled "work table" as two words. Sheraton hyphenated the term ladies' work-table in 1802, and our modern dictionaries spell it as one word, defining a worktable as "a table at which work is done: esp. a small table with drawers, for needlework." The more feminine of the two worktables (29) in the Boscobel collection is a classic example of the "pillar and claw," "astragal end" model with an accordion-pleated silk "bag" below a handsome mahogany case containing compartments for sewing equipment as well as a writing surface. Worktables of this richness and intricacy were the central accoutrement of polite feminine society. At the appropriate time, the ladies of the household would collectively engage themselves with needlework in a sitting room or parlor, or perhaps with writing a note, or reading aloud to each other.

The other, sturdier model of sewing table (30) at Boscobel is also an "astragal end" but on four legs supporting a deep tambour case with side cupboards. It has no elegant intricacies in its interior and may well have been

the more practical worktable which contained the serious sewing and darning of the household.

Chippendale is recorded to have made for the Earl of Pembroke, around 1771, a small drop-leaf table with a drawer and with its leaves supported by brackets in the frame. Since then, that form of table has been called a pembroke, no matter what its style or function. All the New York cabinetmakers' price books called them pembroke tables, the only variation in their list being a "pillar and claw" or pedestal designation as opposed to the standard four-legged models. Their current alternate description as breakfast and library tables is due not only to their usage but to the confusion that arises from the way they have been found listed in inventories of the early nineteenth century. The tables varied greatly in size and served more uses than all other forms.

The earliest of the pembrokes or drop-leaf tables (31) at Boscobel is inlaid with light wood stringing and diamond panels like the New York

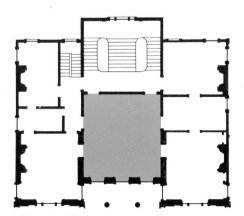

Upstairs Sitting Room.

bureaus by Michael Allison (62, 63). The standard fine model of pembroke made in New York between 1805 and 1820 has four reeded legs with variously shaped leaves.

A rare pair (34) with a Beekman family association has "single elliptical" corners or D-shaped leaves, and the heavier four-legged table (33) has "treble elliptical" leaves like the cluster column or composite "pillar and claw" table (32). The term clover-leaf is frequently used today to describe the more common "double elliptical" leaves on the "pillar and claw" pembroke (35) with a carved urn "pillar."

Candlestands were used essentially for the purpose their name suggests. They were as utilitarian as pembrokes and had as much variety in the shapes of their tops, which usually tilted on a wooden block hinge and were secured by a handsome brass spring bolt catch. It is rare to see a pair (37) such as those at Boscobel, with scroll claws and elliptical or oval tops. The simple urn pedestal, plain claws, and especially the double elliptical top (36) comprise a standard New York form.

26

26 Card tables (pair, treble elliptic).
1805–1810, New York, attributed to
John Dolan by comparison with two
extant labeled card tables, one of which
is in the collection of the Museum of
the City of New York, the other in the
Gracie Mansion Collection, New York.
H.29¼ (74.3) W.36 (91.4) D.17½ (44.5)
Mahogany, tulip poplar, cherry; brass
ferrules.
Purchase, 1976.

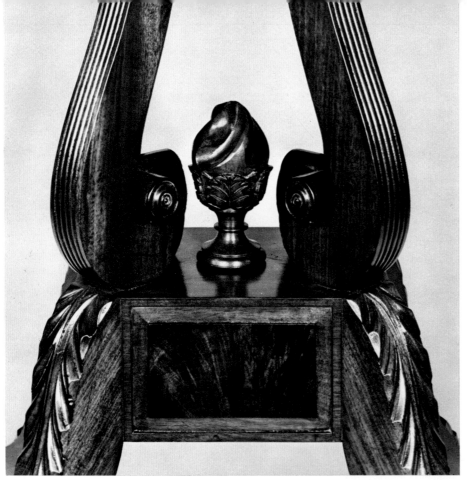

27a

27 Card tables (pair, square with elliptic corners, "D-shaped").
1810–1820, New York, attributed to Duncan Phyfe's workshop.
H.30 (76.2) W.36 (91.4) D.18 (45.7)
Mahogany, tulip poplar, pine; gilt-brass foliate toe caps.
Similar card tables with composite lyreform pedestals are found in the collections of the Albany Institute of History and Art and the Taft Museum, Cincinnati.
Purchase, 1976.

27a Detail of card table.

27

28 Card table, open (pair, treble elliptic).
1810–1820, New York, attributed to
Duncan Phyfe's workshop.
H.28½ (72.4) W.36 (91.4) D.17¾ (45.1)
Mahogany, cherry, tulip poplar, pine;
iron mechanical; ebonized wood paw
feet, brass rollers.
Purchase, 1978.

28a Card table, closed.

28a

28

29

29 Worktable (sewing and writing, square
with astragal ends, pedestal with pleated
silk on frame).
1805–1815, New York, attributed to
Duncan Phyfe's workshop.
H.31½ (80.0) W.24 (61.0) D.12¾ (32.4)
Mahogany, rosewood crossbanding,
tulip poplar, silk; gilt-brass cup casters;
lion-mask knobs.
Purchase, 1976.

30 Worktable (square with astragal ends).
1810–1820, New York, attributed to
Duncan Phyfe's workshop.
H.28 (71.1) W.25⅜ (64.5) D.14⅜ (36.5)
Mahogany, tulip poplar, pine; gilt-brass
paw feet with rollers.
Purchase, 1976.

30

31 Table (drop-leaf, ovolo and serpentine leaves).
1795–1805, New York.
H.28⅝ (72.7) W.20¼ (51.4) leaves down
W.39 (99.1) leaves up D.30¾ (78.1)
Mahogany, tulip poplar, cherry, pine, holly inlays, holly cuffs; oval brass bails.
Purchase, 1961.

32 Table (drop-leaf, treble elliptic, composite: pillar and claw).
1810–1820, New York.
H.29 (73.7) W.24½ (62.2) leaves down
W.49¼ (125.1) leaves up D.36 (91.4)
Mahogany, maple, tulip poplar, pine; gilt-brass lion-mask ring pull and casters.
Underside on medial brace is the 1936 dated label of "H. Ben Pae, Cabinet-maker and Restorer of Antique Furniture, Poughkeepsie, New York."
Purchase, 1976.

33 Table (four-legged, pembroke, treble
elliptic).
1810–1820, New York, possibly by
Charles Christian.
H.29 (73.7) W.24½ (62.2) leaves down
W.46½ (118.1) leaves up D.36 (91.4)
Mahogany, maple, tulip poplar, pine;
gilt-brass cup casters.
A similar table with fluted dies at the
tops of the legs and bearing the label of
Charles Christian of New York is in the
collection of Ronald S. Kane, New York.
Purchase, 1970.

34 Tables (pair, four-legged, pembroke).
1805–1815, New York, Duncan Phyfe.
H.28½ (72.4) W.23⅞ (60.6) leaves down
W.34½ (87.6) leaves up D.45¼ (114.9)
Mahogany, tulip poplar, pine, rosewood
crossbanding; gilt-brass cup casters;
lion-mask knobs.
Beekman family. Under each drawer
rail is a paper sticker with a red border
and diagonal corners which has printed
in ink "BEEKMAN."
Purchase, 1977.

35 Table (drop-leaf, double elliptic, pillar
and claw).
1810–1820, New York.
H.30 (76.2) W.22⅜ (56.8) leaves down
D.35¾ (90.8)
Mahogany, maple, tulip poplar, pine,
ash; gilt-brass rosette knobs and rollers.
Purchase, 1976.

36 Candlestand (tilt-top).
1800–1810, New York.
H.29 (73.7) W.24½ (62.2) D.18⅛ (46.0)
Mahogany, ash block.
Purchase, 1976.

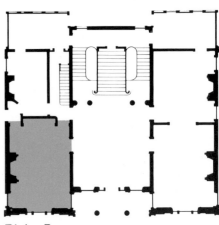

Dining Room.

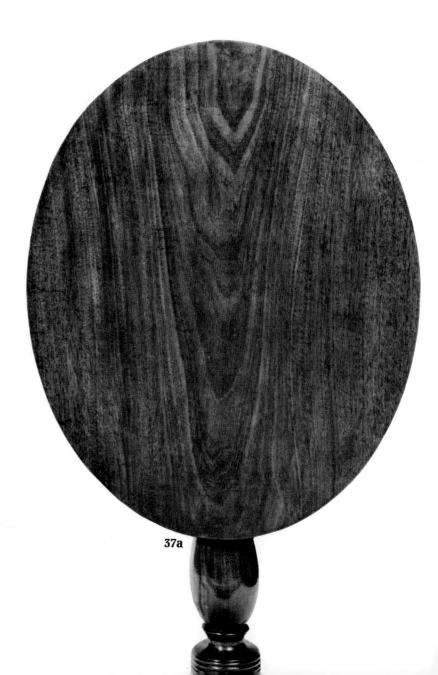

37 Candlestand (pair, tilt-top).
1810–1820, New York.
H.26(66.0) W.23(58.4) D.17¾(45.1)
Mahogany, cherry block and cross-
braces.
Purchase, 1976.

37a Detail of candlestand.

Dining Furniture

The most prominent new forms in Federal period dining rooms were the mahogany sideboards. Hepplewhite wrote in 1788: "The great utility of this piece of furniture has procured it a very general reception; and the conveniences it affords render a dining room incomplete without a sideboard." Robert Adam had commented in 1773: "The eating rooms are considered as apartments of conversation . . . and it is desireable to have them fitted up with elegance and splendor. . . ."

These English ideas of sideboards and dining rooms had become an established tradition in America by the early nineteenth century. In New York, James Fenimore Cooper's description of a Manhattan residence in the 1820's noted a "sideboard, in mahogany, groaning with [silver] plate, knife and spoon cases . . ." and he further remarked, "The eating, or dining-room is almost invariably one of the best in the house. The custom is certainly of English origin, and takes its rise in the habit of sitting an hour or two after the cloth is removed, picking nuts, drinking wine, chatting, yawning, and gazing about the apartment."

An inventory of Joseph Bonaparte's country house at Point Breeze, New Jersey, listed no fewer than three sideboards in his dining room. At Boscobel, there are two handsome New York examples. The earliest of these (38) is in the Hepplewhite taste of serpentine form with square tapered legs inlaid with shells, ellipses, and interlacing traceries with pendant bellflowers. The shield-shaped keyhole escutcheons and quarter-fan inlays on the doors were typical of the best of New York case furniture of the Hepplewhite taste.

The newest fashion at the time of the furnishing of Boscobel was the "pedestal end" Sheraton sideboard (40) with a deep case and short legs. This form was illustrated for the first time as the frontispiece to the New York Price Book of 1810. Federal sideboards like this example often contained several tall drawers with partitions for holding wine bottles.

Related in form and function to this sideboard is the "sideboard table" (39) usually referred to today as a server or serving table. It is an updated version of its eighteenth-century side table prototype before the advent of its larger relative, the sideboard. This example is unusual in having a "hollow front" or slightly concave shape. Both the server and the sideboard have reeded legs ending in brass ferrule feet and "elliptic top" backboards.

The three-part dining tables were ubiquitous in Federal period inventories. Even before the building of Boscobel, States Dyckman's estate inventory of 1806 listed three "mahogany dining tables with ends." Their versatility of form made the tables useful in several areas of a house and they were frequently found in hallways with the ends used as side, or pier, tables. For dining, as many parts as needed for seating could be clamped together or disassembled. They were easily moved about or placed against the wall for sweeping the floor.

Two early three-part dining tables in the Boscobel collection (47, 48) have square tapered legs and half-round ends. The table (47) that descended in the Henderson family is of the plain, sturdy variety. It is unusual in having short, hinged leaves on the ends which appear to be an early nineteenth-century addition designed to increase the seating capacity.

The finest of the dining tables in the Boscobel collection is the great three-part table (43) which stands on twenty reeded legs fitted with brass cup casters. It is analogous in style to the "pedestal end" sideboard (40) and the server (39).

Among the rarities of furniture made for dining and refreshment in the Boscobel collection is a New York Regency-style mahogany wine cooler (42) from the Livingston family. It is lined with zinc and still retains its brass spigot for draining the ice water. The casketlike shape of the case emulates the form of an ancient Roman grave stele or sarcophagus and denotes the then current fascination with archaeological Neo-Classicism which the French called "le style antique."

Even rarer is the tambour, circular, enclosed pillar-and-claw dumbwaiter

(41), which contains a revolving frame of three shelves for wine glasses or tea cups. Only two other similar examples are known, one of which is in the Winterthur collection. Although the form is not to be found in the New York price books, it has numerous precedents in English Regency dumbwaiters and book racks. On the top are two original metal pins, which may have stabilized a fitted mahogany or Sheffield gallery tray, now missing.

Larger than a tilt-top candlestand, but smaller than New York breakfast tables of similar form, is the pillar-and-claw tea table (44). It is believed to have been made in the workshop of Phyfe about 1817 for Stephen Van Rensselaer, in whose family it remained until very recently. The character of the superb carving on the pedestal relates closely to the Phyfe card tables (27). The solid mahogany tilt-top with "single elliptic corners" is richly grained in plum-pudding configurations, which contribute to the masterpiece quality of this table made at the height of Duncan Phyfe's career.

Equally fine and unusual is the Phyfe mahogany urn stand (45) made to support what was undoubtedly a classical Sheffield hot water or tea urn with spigot. An inset marble top framed in cherry wood protected the richly figured mahogany veneers of the drawer facade from water damage.

Mahogany butler's trays and stands are found listed in all the New York price books from 1796 through 1817, as well as in the earliest nineteenth-century inventories, including that of Dyckman. Perhaps because of their heavy usage and vulnerability, American survivals are seldom seen. The butler's tray and stand (46) in the Boscobel collection emerged only recently from under the eaves of the attic of a Hudson River Federal period homestead, where it had survived the ravages of recent generations. It fits the descriptions of the New York price books perfectly.

A hinged oval window in the sideboard alcove provides visibility and ventilation from the butler's pantry.

38 Sideboard (serpentine).
1795–1805, New York.
H.42¾ (108.6) W.69½ (176.6) D.28 (71.1)
Mahogany, tulip poplar, pine, satinwood
and holly inlays.
Purchase, 1970.

39 Sideboard table, "server" (concave).
1805–1815, New York, possibly by
Michael Allison.
H.36 (91.4) to top of splashboard
W.35 5/16 (89.7) D.19 3/4 (50.2)
Mahogany, ebony banding, tulip poplar,
pine; gilt-brass lion-mask knobs and
ferrules.
The small center "tablet" drawer is
similar in plan to that in the 1810 bureau
labeled by Michael Allison in the collection of the Metropolitan Museum of Art.
Purchase, 1976.

39a Side view of table.

39a

40 Sideboard (pedestal end).
1810, New York.
H.53 (134.6) W.76¼ (193.7) D.28 (71.1)
Mahogany, pine, tulip poplar; gilt-brass
lion-mask ring pulls and ferrule feet.
Purchase, 1976.

40

41

41 Dumbwaiter.
1810–1820, New York, attributed to
Duncan Phyfe's workshop.
H.44 (111.8) Diam.24 (61.0)
Mahogany, tulip poplar, pine; gilt-brass
rosette knobs and paw feet with rollers.
Purchase, 1976.

42 Cellarette.
1810–1820, New York, attributed to
Duncan Phyfe's workshop.
H.23½ (59.7) W.26³⁄₁₆ (66.5) D.22³⁄₁₆ (56.3)
Mahogany, pine; zinc lining, brass
spigot; gilt-brass cup casters.
From Callendar House.
Purchase, 1976.

42

68

43

43 Dining table (3-part with elliptic ends).
1810–1815, New York, attributed to
Duncan Phyfe's workshop.
H.29(73.7) W.53½(135.9)
Center: L.71¾(182.3) leaves up
D.24½(62.2) leaves down
Ends: D.24½(62.2)
Mahogany, pine, tulip poplar, rosewood
crossbanding; gilt-brass cup casters.
Purchase, 1976.

44

44b

44a

45a

44 Table (tilt-top, tea or center).
1817, New York, Duncan Phyfe.
H.29(73.7) W.42(106.7) D.27½(69.9)
Mahogany throughout; gilt-brass foli-
ated toe caps with rollers.
Descended in the family of Stephen Van
Rensselaer, the seventh Patroon. Illus-
trated in Nancy McClelland, *Duncan
Phyfe and the English Regency* (New
York: William R. Scott, 1939), p. 303,
plate 292.
Purchase, 1977.

44a Detail of table.

44b Table with tilted top.

45 Urn stand.
1810–1820, New York, Duncan Phyfe.
H.30(76.2) W.17¼(43.8) D.17¼(43.8)
Mahogany, cherry, brass, ivory, tulip
poplar, pine; gray mottled marble
(replaced); ivory pendants; gilt-brass
rosette knobs; paw feet with rollers.
Descended in the Ludlow family.
Purchase, 1976.

45a Detail of urn stand.

45

46 Butler's tray (waiter).
1800–1820, New York, Hudson Valley.
Tray: H.4¾ (12.1) W.34 (86.4)
D.21 (53.3)
Stand: H.27¾ (70.5) open
H.36 (91.4) closed W.22 (55.9)
Mahogany throughout.
Purchase, 1977.

46

47

47 Dining table (3-part with elliptic ends).
1790–1810, New York.
H.28½ (72.4) W.55½ (141.0)
Center: L.70½ (179.1) leaves up
D.24½ (62.2) leaves down
Ends: D.27 (68.6) Extra leaf: D.8½ (21.6)
Mahogany, tulip poplar.
Descended in the Henderson family.
Purchase, 1976.

48 Dining table (3-part with elliptic ends).
1790–1800, New York.
H.28¼ (71.8) W.48 (121.9)
Center: D.63 (160.0) leaves up
D.22¼ (56.5) leaves down
Ends: D.23 (58.4)
Mahogany, holly, tulip poplar, ash.
Purchase, 1976.

48

Depending upon the needs and the means of the client, the American cabinetmakers of the Federal period could supply a variety of types of beds. The current expression "four poster" applied to what was then called a "high post bedstead." Together with its bed hangings, the high post bedstead was usually the richest and most important of the bedsteads in a home. It was generally seven feet or more in height.

The simplest beds were called "cott bedsteads." Their tapered or turned foot posts averaged two feet in height and protruded only slightly above the rail. Today, these are referred to as "attic beds" for they were often set up there to accomodate servants and an overflow of guests. The "cott bedsteads" were mortised and tenoned like all other poster beds, but were invariably not bolted. They were secured by ropes, which, when tightly laced through holes in the rails and tied to the posts, held the bed together.

In gradation, the next higher form was the "low post bedstead" usually bolted together and averaging about four feet in height. The tops of the posts were turned in variant finial forms and were never intended to receive a canopy frame. The headposts held, by mortise and tenon joints, a shaped headboard which supported bolsters or pillows.

The same construction was used in the next highest form, the "field bedstead," with posts averaging about five and a half feet tall. These were designed expressly to receive an arched canopy frame for curtains. On New York field beds the frame was usually a simple elliptic form. The term "field bed" was explained by Sheraton, who wrote, "they receive this name on account of their being similar in size and shape to those really used in camps. . . ." In America, the field bedstead was often the best bed in modest homes with low ceilings, and was favored in the more elegant establishments for younger members of the family and house guests.

In the Boscobel collection is a handsome Sheraton mahogany field bed (51) with the foot posts turned in a typical New York profile of an elongated urn and circular spade foot. Both the headboard and frame are "elliptic." The pure white curtains, so favored in the Federal period, are of sheer cotton fabric called "mull," somewhat like modern batiste. They could easily be closed in summer months for protection from insects and gave the bed some importance by its fashionable dressing.

Similarly treated was the crib or infant's bed (53) of related form. Instead of a headboard it had turned baluster guard rails on all sides. One long side opened downward on hinges and was secured by inset brass thumb-nail spring bolts at each end of the top rail.

The other three beds in the Boscobel collection are all "high post bedsteads" of different types. The earlier and plainer of these beds is today called a "pencil post" (54) because of its slender, tapering octagonal posts. It was a common form in America from the early eighteenth century through the early nineteenth century. Most of these were made of native woods painted either red, blue, black, or green. The Boscobel example has maple posts and a pine headboard. It is painted dark green and very likely resembles one of several green high post beds mentioned in the Dyckman estate inventory of 1806. Here the curtains are of the simplest style, reproducing the hand-loomed blue-and-white-checked linen fabric so popular in the Hudson Valley.

The most important beds in the collection are the two carved mahogany high post beds (49, 50), the first of which (49), with its fine reeding, stop fluting, drapery, leaves and rosette blocks (49A), ranks in quality at the top of those few known to be from the workshop of Duncan Phyfe. The silk bed hangings are appropriately adapted from the elaborate schemes of Shera-ton's design plates in keeping with the richness of the bed and its mahogany cornice.

The other high post bed in the Boscobel collection has posts with a profile of slightly later date. It is also of Phyfe quality in its crisply carved leaves and the wheat spears skillfully intersticed between the reeds of the

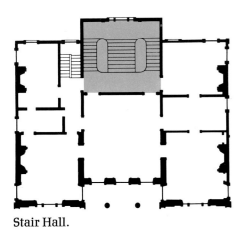

Stair Hall.

upper posts (50A). This bed is hung with a fringed dimity, a striped, white cotton much like today's seersucker cloth. It was the favorite fabric of the Federal period, admired by George Washington for its whiteness; it was even used for the ballroom curtains in Mount Vernon.

The sleeping level of nineteenth-century high post beds was often quite elevated by the time they were made up with down-filled ticking over a hair mattress. In some cases, mahogany bedsteps or library steps were provided to aid the young and infirm in getting into bed. In the Boscobel collection, an ingenious set of New York steps (52) contains a chamber pot board or "night convenience." The center step, which conceals a frame that slides forward on the lower step, has a hinged tread that serves as a cover and a backrest (52A). This kind of inventive mechanical disguise is characteristic of the concepts espoused in the English design books of both Shearer and Sheraton.

A wooden rocking horse stands near a New York field bed in the guest room.

49 Bedstead (high post with cornice).
1805–1810, New York, attributed to
Duncan Phyfe's workshop.
H.100½ (255.3) L.77¾ (197.5) W.59¾ (151.8)
Bedstead mahogany throughout; cor-
nice mahogany and mahogany veneer
on white pine; green silk curtains.
Descended in the Tathum family of
New York.
Bed: purchase, 1977; cornice: gift of
Thomas Kyle, 1977.

49a Detail of carving on foot posts.

49

49a

50

50a

50 Bedstead (high post).
1810–1820, New York, Duncan Phyfe's
workshop.
H.95 (241.3) L.78 (198.1) W.59¾ (151.8)
Mahogany throughout; gilt-brass
collars and rollers; white striped dimity
curtains.
Purchase, 1976.

50a Detail of carving on all four posts.

51 Bedstead (field).
1805–1810, New York.
H.82½ (209.6) L.78¼ (198.8) W.54¼
(137.8)
Mahogany; maple rails; white mull
curtains.
Purchase, 1977.

52 Bed steps with commode.
1810–1820, New York.
H.24½ (62.2) W.19 (48.3) D.24 (61.0)
Mahogany, tulip poplar, pine; gilt-brass
ferrules.
The steps are inset with an early
nineteenth-century Brussels carpet.
Purchase, 1977.

52a Bed steps opened to commode.

51

52

52a

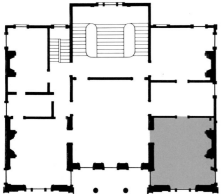

Elizabeth Dyckman's Chamber.

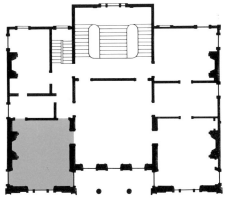

Peter Corne Dyckman's Chamber.

53

53 Child's crib (field).
1810, New York.
H.66½ (168.9) L.47½ (120.7) W.23⅝ (60.0)
Mahogany throughout; white mull curtains.
Purchase, 1964.

54 Bedstead (high post, "pencil" type).
1780–1800, American.
H.72¾ (184.8) L.83¼ (211.5) W.59¼ (150.5)
Maple, pine, painted green; blue-and-white-checked linen curtains.
Purchase, 1977.

54

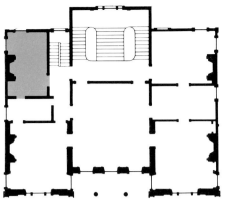

Sill's Room.

Basin Stands and Dressing Tables

Wash stands or "wash hand stands," as they are sometimes listed in early nineteenth-century household inventories, were called "bason stands" in *The Journeymen Cabinet and Chair Makers' Book of Prices* for New York in 1796 and 1810. The stands were available in a variety of forms and degrees of elaboration. They were either square, corner, or circular and were either open or enclosed. They all had a "bason hole" and "cup holes." The larger, center hole was to secure the washbasin while in use, and the smaller, adjacent holes were to hold containers for soap and toothbrushes. Basin stands were generally placed near a window in bedchambers and dressing rooms. They were occasionally found in the dining room, as noted in an 1817 room-by-room inventory of Stephen Decatur's home in the Capitol City of Washington.

The most popular basins and pitchers were made of English pottery such as creamware and stoneware, or of Chinese export porcelain with a matching water bottle and stopper. The pitcher or bottle stood on the open, lower shelf or in the cupboard below while the basin was in use. The toilet accoutrement which furnished a basin stand was often purchased "en suite" as it likely was on June 20, 1808, when Elizabeth Dyckman "Bot of Wm Hewitt, New York, 1 Grecian Patern Ewer & Bowl, 1 Chamber & Cover, 1 Soap Box & Brush tray."

All of the basin stands in the Boscobel collection have the classic New York turning of the legs with the characteristic foot. The two early corner models (55, 57) have elegantly shaped high splash boards to protect the walls from water spray. Figure 55 is completely enclosed below with a cupboard door and sham drawers. Both corner stands have a front center leg to prevent them from falling forward when in use. The standard square enclosed New York basin stand (56), of which there are many survivals, has the distinguishing enrichment of brass paw feet. Most elegant and costly were the square basin stands (59) fitted with casters and enclosed with an elliptic tambour shutter. The only other example known to date is in the collection of the Metropolitan Museum of Art.

Dressing tables, like most basin stands, were strictly bed chamber and dressing room furniture. In the Boscobel collection are two fine examples (58, 61) with a dressing glass fixed to the top. The table (58) with two small handkerchief drawers mounted on the top and spanned by a swinging glass is the first occurrence of a design concept that was applied to all styles of Classical dressing bureaus and later dressers made in America throughout the nineteenth century. Its evolution in New York is clearly analogous to the "pedestal end" sideboard (40) with an identical arrangement of surface-mounted drawers connected by an elliptic backboard. The linings of the small drawers of this dressing table are of mahogany, as are many of those in the small case pieces made in the best Federal period workshops of urban centers like New York. The perfect quality of execution and the careful selection and arrangement of figured mahogany veneers plus other details warrant the attribution of this dressing table to the workshop of Duncan Phyfe.

The other New York dressing table (61) reflects the English Regency taste for curule legs like those of the Phyfe drawing room furniture at Boscobel. The stretcher is carved in double-reversed twisted reeding frequently used by 1815 on bed posts and table legs. The spade feet are a carry-over from the earlier Hepplewhite style and were often used by the later New York cabinetmakers as "therms" on spider-leg candlestands in lieu of the more costly paw feet or casters. The carved lyre or cyma scroll brackets which support the glass are like those on several known labeled examples of dressing tables by Michael Allison, but this dressing table could have been made in any one of the best workshops, including that of Phyfe.

Related in function is the portable "toilet looking glass" (60) bearing the label of Ambrose Crane, who ran a short-lived looking-glass store at 185 Broadway from 1817 to 1819. It is evident from his advertisement in the

New York Evening Post of September 24, 1817, that he was strictly a retailer and not a cabinetmaker as was his contemporary, Hosea Dugliss, who advertised "for sale at less than auction prices . . . Mantel, Pier and Toilet Looking Glasses, of his own manufacture. . . ." A cheval glass of similar form, bearing the label of Dugliss, indicates that he may have been the maker of the Boscobel toilet glass sold by Crane. This glass, cheap and expedient, and without a case of drawers, could easily be used on any table and at best would transform the plainest typical New York bureau of the period into a handsome dressing bureau.

A small office, named for States Dyckman's ward, States Brewer, contains country furnishings from New York and New England, including a Federal painted and grained basin stand.

55 Basin stand (corner, enclosed).
1800–1810, New York.
H.46½ (118.1) W.26(66.0) D.18⅜ (46.7)
Mahogany, tulip poplar, maple; gilt-brass lion-mask knobs.
Purchase, 1977.

55

56

57

56 Basin stand (square, enclosed).
1805–1810, New York.
H.36 (91.4)   W.15¾ (40.0)   D.15¾ (40.0)
Mahogany, tulip poplar, pine; gilt-brass
rosette knobs and paw feet.
Purchase, 1977.

57 Basin stand (corner).
1800–1810, New York.
H.48 (121.9)   W.24⅜ (61.9)   D.17⅝ (44.8)
Mahogany, tulip poplar, pine; gilt-brass
circular bail.
Purchase, 1977.

59

58

58 Dressing table ("chamber table").
1810, New York, attributed to Duncan
Phyfe.
H.64½ (163.8) W.41 (104.1) D.20½ (52.1)
Mahogany and mahogany drawer
lining, tulip poplar, pine; gilt-brass
lion-mask knobs and ferrule feet.
Illustrated in Edgar G. Miller, Jr.,
American Antique Furniture (New
York: M. Barrows & Company, 1937),
vol. 1, p. 417, fig. 755.
Purchase, 1977.

59 Basin stand (tambour, enclosed).
1805–1810, New York.
H.35½ (90.2) W.18⅝ (47.3) D.18 (45.7)
Mahogany, tulip poplar, pine; gilt-brass
rosette knobs and cup casters.
An engraved calling card tacked on
inside of drawer front reads
"Mr. Jonathan C. Pierce."
Purchase, 1977.

60 Dressing glass.
1818–1819, New York.
Labeled: "Ambrose Crane,/Importer and
Manufacturer/of/Prints/and/Looking
Glasses,/No. 185/Broadway, New York/
Near the City Hotel."
H.21 (53.3) W.19 (48.3) D.10¾ (27.3)
Mahogany, pine; brass finials and
thumbscrews.
Purchase, 1977.

60a Label of Ambrose Crane.

60a

61

60

61 Dressing table (curule).
1810–1820, New York.
H.55 (139.7) W.37 (94.0) D.19⅛ (48.6)
Mahogany, tulip poplar, pine; gilt-brass
rosette knobs.
Purchase, 1977.

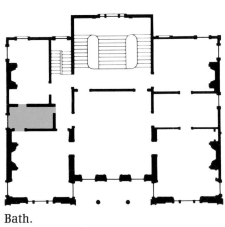

Bath.

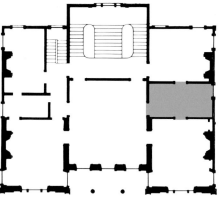

Dressing Room.

Bureaus and Wardrobes

At the time of the building of Boscobel, the storage of clothing was still quite different from today. Closets with hanging arrangements, as we know them, were nonexistent. Night clothes, robes, and coats might be hung on hooks or pegs in shallow closets, but all other clothing was neatly folded and stored in drawers, on shelves, or in chests. The wardrobe and the chest of drawers, or "bureau" as it was called, which had developed from the simple chest of the seventeenth century, remained important forms in the Classical period. Not until the middle of the nineteenth century did it occur to architects and builders that their new designs for "cottages" and "villas," with asymmetrical floor plans, allowed spaces for large closets and other such conveniences.

In New York from 1800 to 1810, a distinctive model of bureaus evolved with a deep top drawer, called by the cabinetmakers a "tablet drawer." This deep drawer was intended for the storage of bulky materials such as coverlets and blankets. Since the late nineteenth century, the drawer has been called by antiquarians and furniture enthusiasts a blanket drawer, relating it in thought and use to its earlier prototype, the blanket chest, which had a deep upper compartment and a hinged lid. In the eyes of the cabinetmaker of Neo-Classical New York, the deep drawer became the frieze of an entablature analagous in concept to the tablet and cornice of an architectural looking glass or mantelpiece. Accordingly, he treated this visually awkward space with currently fashionable, decorative veneer patterns and inlays, making it a focal point of the entire bureau.

Two perfect examples of this are seen in the Boscobel collection in the early bureaus of the prominent New York cabinetmaker Michael Allison. One of these (62) bears his printed paper label, showing his address at 42 Vesey Street, where he first opened shop in 1800. He remained there until 1816 when he moved to 50 Vesey Street. Numerous labeled examples of similar Allison bureaus have appeared and disappeared on the market in the last twenty years. Like the Boscobel examples, they all have eagle brasses and satinwood diamond panels, either striped or plain, and variously inlaid with a rose, lily of the valley, eagle, shell, or feather and cross.

It seems significant that all the labeled bureaus with "tablet drawers" with this type of decoration were marked Allison. It is possible that this decorative tablet scheme was one of his own design. Certainly the basic form of the bureau itself was made by other New York cabinetmakers. It had become a standard in the Price Book by 1810, when the elegantly splayed feet and characteristic double lobed apron were called "French feet and drapery." An example of the most basic form in the Price Book with few "extras" is the unusually low and plain example without the "tablet drawer" in the Boscobel collection (64).

Between 1810 and 1817, another distinctive form of New York bureau became the standard of the cabinetmakers. The new form, called a "dressing bureau," usually contained a "tablet drawer" often topped by a range of two or three small drawers. A dressing glass (60) without its own drawers could be placed on it at a convenient level. The basic differences in the new bureaus were a new taste for the Sheraton style in turned feet and reeding, and the disappearance of the light wood stringing and bail drawer pulls.

In the Boscobel collection are two fine examples. One (65) lacks the "tablet drawer" but has four graduated full-width drawers below two smaller ones. Its elegant proportions and ovolo reeded corner posts give it a slightly earlier feeling than the other bureau (66) with the "tablet drawer." This heavier bureau is nearly identical to three others labeled about 1815 by Michael Allison, one of which is in the collection of the Museum of the City of New York.

Since the days of Dutch settlement in the Hudson Valley, the wardrobe, or Kas as the Dutch called it, was a major piece of furniture in any prosperous home. Like those of European origin, the Kas was a massive construction distinguished by its paneled doors, giant cornice, and ball feet. It remained popular here with the Dutch settlers and their descendants into the early nineteenth century. Its typical eighteenth-century Anglo-American counterpart is seen in the Boscobel example (67), which very likely resembles the "mahogany wardrobe" listed in the Dyckman estate inventory of 1806. This wardrobe is nearly identical to another example, at the New-York Historical Society, bearing the label of Thomas Burling, the father of a prominent Beekman Street family of cabinetmakers working in New York from 1787 to 1802. Behind the paneled doors are typical sliding trays, similar in form to the mahogany waiter (46). The Chippendale style of its case, with bracket feet and molded cornice, was retardataire in that, like the Dutch Kas, it carried the taste of previous generations into a new period. The only details that clearly reveal its Federal period origin are the brass keyhole liners and the richly figured mahogany veneers on the frieze of its cornice.

By 1810, the New York price books listed a new standard form, the "French Wardrobe," with full-length doors. In the Boscobel collection are two very similar examples (68, 69), attributed to the emigré Charles-Honoré Lannuier. Both are fitted with imported French locks and hinges and have a characteristic French aspect except for the legs, which have typical New York Sheraton turnings.

Until recent years, the wardrobes had stood for generations in Callendar House, one of the many Livingston family seats. The Livingstons were known to have been patrons of the French cabinetmaker Lannuier, and the Chancellor himself had earlier brought furniture from Paris to New York.

The zenith of American wardrobes in the Boscobel collection is the "winged wardrobe" (70) attributed to the workshop of Duncan Phyfe. In the New York Price Book of 1810 it was, with the winged bookcase, the most expensive piece of furniture of its time. In this rare example are seen all of the finest elements of Phyfe's work in design and carving. The tablet of the frieze has the carved rosettes, drapery (70A), and thunderbolt motifs seen on Phyfe's sofas and chairs. On the door panels, a studied arrangement of densely figured mahogany flame veneers soars upward as in a holocaust and gives a note of excitement to an otherwise sober, but perfectly elegant, expression of the master.

Carved thunderbolts and bow knots embellish a "winged wardrobe" from the workshop of Duncan Phyfe.

62 Bureau.
1800–1805, New York, Michael Allison.
Labeled: "M. Allison/Cabinetmaker/
NO. 42 Vesey Street/ (NEAR THE BEAR
MARKET) /NEW-YORK/Who has a gen-
eral assortment of warranted/ready
made Furniture on Hand." Original eagle
and garland bail brasses stamped "H. J."
H.45 (114.3) W.45½ (115.6) D.22¾ (57.8)
Mahogany, satinwood, holly, tulip
poplar, pine.
Purchase, 1977.

62a Label of Michael Allison.

62

63

63a

63 Bureau.
1800–1805, New York, attributed to
Michael Allison.
H.45⅝ (115.9) W.45¼ (114.9) D.22¼
(56.5)
Mahogany, satinwood, holly, tulip pop-
lar, pine; original eagle bail brasses
stamped ''H. J.''
Descended in the Henderson family.
Purchase, 1962.

63a Detail of top drawer, rosebud inlay.

64

65

64 Bureau (low).
1800–1805, New York, possibly by
Michael Allison.
H.37⅞ (96.2) W.43¼ (109.9) D.22 (55.9)
Mahogany, tulip poplar, pine; gilt-brass
oval bails.
From the Fulton-Ludlow
House, Claverack, New York.
Purchase, 1976.

65 Bureau.
1805–1810, New York, attributed to
Michael Allison.
H.47¾ (121.3) W.45½ (115.6) D.22½
(57.2)
Mahogany, tulip poplar, pine; gilt-brass
rosette knobs and ferrules.
Purchase, 1976.

66 Bureau.
1810–1815.
H.48¾ (123.8) W.46¼ (117.5) D.22⅝
(57.5)
Mahogany, tulip poplar, pine; gilt-brass
lion-mask knobs and ferrules.
Purchase, 1976.

66

67

67 Wardrobe (English-form).
1780–1800, New York, attributed to
Thomas Burling.
H.87½ (222.3) W.55¼ (140.3) D.24 (61.0)
Mahogany, mahogany veneer, tulip
poplar; gilt-brass bails.
From the Fulton-Ludlow House,
Claverack, New York.
Purchase, 1976.

68 Wardrobe ("French").
1805–1810, New York, attributed to
Charles-Honoré Lannuier.
H.83½ (212.1) W.54½ (138.4) D.20¾
(52.7)
Mahogany, tulip poplar, pine;
turning of leg emulates a brass ferrule in
mahogany.
Descended in the Livingston family
(from Callendar House).
Similar to fig. 69.
Purchase, 1977.

69 Wardrobe ("French").
1805–1810, New York, attributed to
Charles-Honoré Lannuier.
H.83½ (212.1) W.54½ (138.4) D.20¾
(52.7)
Mahogany, tulip poplar, pine;
turning of leg is a typical New York
form (standard).
Descended in the Livingston family
(from Callendar House).
Similar to fig. 68.
Purchase, 1976.

68

69

70a

70 Wardrobe (winged).
1810–1815, New York, Duncan Phyfe's workshop.
H.65¾ (167.0) W.61 (154.9) D.22½ (57.2)
Mahogany, tulip poplar, pine; gilt-brass ferrules.
Purchase, 1976.

70a Detail of carved tablets on frieze.

70

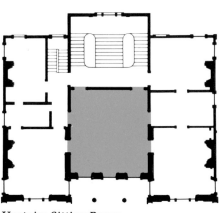

Upstairs Sitting Room.

Writing Tables, Desks, and Bookcases

The gentry of Federal America was often well informed and highly literate, and spent a considerable number of hours in reading and in writing letters. Those who could afford books accumulated their own reference libraries. States Dyckman had an impressive collection of 1,400 volumes, which were preserved by successive generations of Livingston family owners. A number of the books are now appropriately exhibited at Boscobel in the period bookcases which will be discussed later.

The range of subjects contained in a gentleman's library was often very broad, including especially history, philosophy, religion, geography, astronomy, classical mythology, agriculture, and botany. In a day when handmade bindings were an everyday occurrence, the books were invariably covered in handsome calfskin and Moroccan leathers, embellished with decorative gilt borders. Arranged on the shelves of mahogany bookcases, they made a splendid appearance behind glazed doors.

The personal letter was the only method of long-distance communication between families, friends, and business associates. When writing letters, the penman nearly always made record copies which, in the extended interim period of sending and receiving mail, could be recalled to memory. At the same time, there was a distinctly self-conscious preservation of correspondence which became family record. It is from the letters that have survived that much of our American history has been written. This is certainly the case with States and Elizabeth Dyckman, whose surviving letters and papers number over 1,300 items.

The cabinetmakers of Federal New York could provide a wide variety of handsome furniture designed specifically for writing and the convenient storage of books and written records. In the Boscobel collection are two extraordinary writing tables. The more impressive of these is the "circular pillar and claw library writing table" (71), as it was called in the price books. In current vernacular it is usually referred to as a drum table by virtue of its shape. Its identity as a writing surface has been obscured in this century by a preponderance of popular factory-made reproductions of the form, not intended for that purpose.

In this example the top is inset with an octagonal green wool baize and trimmed with a leather border of a gilt Greek fret on a red ground. It is an exact copy of the deteriorated original. All-over leather was seldom used on New York library tables, although it was listed as a specific alternate to cloth as early as the Price Book of 1796. Historically, this table is of particular interest in that it belonged to James Kirke Paulding. According to family tradition, it was on this table that he wrote his famous *Salmagundi* papers.

The other writing table (73) in the Boscobel collection is diminutive and portable by comparison. In the price books it was called a "pillar and claw rising top writing table" and in this instance resembles a "square work table" with "hollow corners." It bears the label of Joel Curtis (73A), 153 Chamber Street, New York, his address from 1817 to 1820. The style of the acanthus leaf carving on the pedestal is not typical of New York, and is more closely related to Philadelphia work.

Among the major masterpieces of furniture in the Boscobel collection is the "library book-case with wings" (72). The current name for this form is breakfront. It was the single most costly creation of the cabinetmakers' skill in its day, and contains, in its detailing, nearly every possible "extra" in the New York Price Book of 1810. The "tablets" of the cornice are carved in the classical Phyfe manner with the central tablet bearing the bookplate arms of a prominent New Yorker, Thomas Witter Chrystie, for whom this bookcase was made. It is thought to be the first piece of American furniture to bear a coat of arms in its design.

As in the best desks, the interior facade of the writing compartment is lined with satinwood and the small interior drawer knobs are turned from ivory. The lower case is fully reeded around its top edge and down the stiles to the turned legs, which are carved with pendant water leaves and terminate in brass ferrules. Of the twenty-eight patterns illustrated in the price books, this Gothic tracery of the glazed doors was the one most often used for bookcases by the New York cabinet-makers, especially Duncan Phyfe.

A simpler version of Gothic doors is seen on the small secretary, or "lady's cabinet" (74), which is believed to have been made by Phyfe and which once stood at Mount Gulian, the Hudson River seat of the Verplanck family. The writing surface is a hinged "flap" which, when open, rests on the extended drawer below. The original lion-head gilt-brass drawer pulls and ferrule feet are the typical fittings found on the best of Sheraton mahogany furniture made in New York between 1810 and 1820.

A small secretary, or "lady's cabinet," stands between the windows in Mrs. Dyckman's chamber. Attributed to the workshop of Duncan Phyfe, it descended in the prominent Verplanck family.

103

71 Library table (circular).
1810–1815, New York, attributed to
Duncan Phyfe's workshop.
H.29¾ (75.6) Diam.59¼ (150.5)
Mahogany, tulip poplar, white pine;
gilt-brass mock handles; green baize
with gilt-embossed red leather tape;
gilt-brass paw feet with rollers.
Descended in the family of James Kirke
Paulding, for whom it was made.
Purchase, 1978.

72 Bookcase (winged, with desk).
1810–1820, New York, attributed to
Duncan Phyfe's workshop.
H.94½ (240.0) W.78½ (199.4)
Center: D.16⅝ (42.2)
Wings: D.14⅝ (37.2)
Mahogany, satinwood, tulip poplar,
pine; gilt-brass lion-mask knobs and
ferrules.
Illustrated in Parke-Bernet Galleries,
Inc., Sale Catalogue #1028, January 13,
14, 15, 1949, pp. 90, 91, lot 436.
Descended in the family of Thomas
Witter Chrystie, New York attorney,
through William Few Chrystie.
Purchase, 1977.

72a Detail of central tablet of bookplate
arms of Thomas Witter Chrystie.
Earliest known piece of American
furniture with a coat of arms in its
design. Described in Charles Knowles
Bolton, *Bolton's American Armory*
(Boston: F. W. Faxon Company, 1927),
p. 34.

72a

71

73a

73

73 Writing table.
1821–1823, New York, Joel Curtis.
Labeled: "J. CURTIS/CABINETMAKER/
153/Chamber Street/NEW YORK."
H.33 (83.8) W.22¼ (56.5) D.16 (40.6)
Mahogany, tulip poplar, pine; gilt-brass
lion-mask ring pulls and paw feet with
rollers.
Illustrated in Nancy McClelland,
Duncan Phyfe and the English Regency
(New York: William R. Scott, 1939),
pp. 199–200, plates 183 and 184.
Purchase, 1976.

73a Label of Joel Curtis.

74 Desk and bookcase.
1810, New York, attributed to Duncan
Phyfe's workshop.
H.75 (190.5) W.43⅝ (110.8) D.20⅛ (51.1)
Mahogany, tulip poplar, pine; gilt-brass
lion-mask ring pulls and ferrules.
Descended in the Verplanck family
through Mrs. Gertrude Kneveles.
Purchase, 1977.

74

107

Looking Glasses, Clocks, Fire Screens, and Chandeliers

In Federal America, all flat, silvered, reflecting glasses that were framed and hung on the wall were called looking glasses. The term "mirror," which is in general use today, originally referred specifically to what is still called a convex mirror. The carvers and gilders who made convex mirrors sometimes called them "cornice mirrors," since the design of their frames was essentially the cornice detail of an architectural looking glass modified to surround a circular or an oval glass (77, 79).

The records show that large numbers of framed looking glasses were imported to America from both England and the Continent well into the nineteenth century. By 1790, American looking-glass makers were advertising glasses of their own make along with imported examples. Most plate glass was imported until the mid-nineteenth century, since the American glass houses seemingly could not produce, in quantity, large plates of glass of the unwavering quality needed for silvering. When Henry Bradshaw Fearon visited New York in 1817, he noted in his well-known diary "that there are here several large carvers' and gilders' shops. Glass mirrors and picture frames are executed with taste and elegance, but still the most superior are imported from England. Carved ornaments are general, though some composition ornaments are used. Plateglass is imported from France, Holland and England, the latter bearing the highest price."

The earliest style of Federal looking glass in the Boscobel collection has a frame of mahogany veneer over white pine with carved and gilded ornaments. It is a distinctly American type (75) peculiar to New York and the Hudson Valley. It combines the Chippendale taste in its swan's neck pediment; the Hepplewhite taste in line inlays, Classical rosettes, garlands, and urn with floral sprays; and the Sheraton taste in its églomisé tablets. The basic architectural form has English Georgian precedents which predate Chippendale and Hepplewhite.

A related looking glass, in the collection of Sleepy Hollow Restorations, bears a stenciled label which reads: "From Del Vecchio Looking Glass & Picture Frame Manufacturers, New York." John and Joseph Del Vecchio were in partnership in New York from 1805 to 1814, and it may well have been from them that Stephen and Abigail Young bought the looking glass in Boscobel's collection on July 7, 1807.

In the first two decades of the nineteenth century, architectural looking glasses with pillared frames, cornices, and ornamented tablets were the most prevalent. In the Boscobel collection is a handsome pair of looking glasses (76) which would have been called pier glasses by virtue of their great size. They descended in the prominent Massachusetts family of Joseph Tilden (portraits of Tilden and his wife are among the paintings in Boscobel's collection), and the profiles of their molded cornices, their all-over tight design, and the careful placement of the decorative elements are characteristic of the Boston area and especially of the great workshop of John Doggett of Roxbury. Doggett's records show that his looking glasses, and materials for making them, were sent to Albany and New York City, among numerous distant places.

Even greater in size than the pair of pier glasses is the overmantel looking glass or "Chimney glass" (80). It is definitely of American origin, from either Boston or New York, although as yet there are no clear analogies to documented examples to be drawn from its all-over detail. The designs of its elegant églomisé panels are clearly from the mode of Adam and Hepplewhite.

Another pair of pier glasses in the Boscobel collection (78) is more closely identified with English looking glasses. Their design, which is essentially that of a delicate rectangular picture frame molding surmounted by ornaments of eagle and drapery, is a modified composite of plates 116 and 117 from Hepplewhite's *Guide* of 1788 and 1795. The eagle and drapery motifs were also favorite decorative elements of the New York carvers. Carved drapery is found not only on much of the New York furniture in the Boscobel collection but

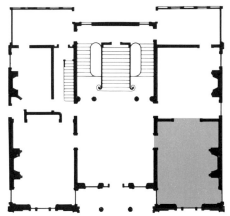

Front Drawing Room.

on the house itself, between the pillars of its upper loggia. A single pier glass of similar form (81) has a heavier picture frame molding with ornament frequently seen on New York portraits of the late 1810's and early 1820's.

Convex mirrors are among the most difficult Federal looking glasses to identify as being of English or American origin. By 1800, they were being imported in quantity and sold by the New York carvers and gilders along with their own products. The carvers followed closely the English models, and even modern-day wood analysis does not conclusively determine their origin because of the American exportation of pine and other problems. Some examples, bearing the labels of American stores, were often sold, but not made, by the vendors.

Convex mirrors usually came in pairs and were intended to light a room as well as to provide stylish symmetrical ornament for its walls. In the Boscobel collection is a pair of small circular convex mirrors with "lights" (77). The eagle perched upon rocks and the acanthus leaf pendant are typical ornaments, as is the reeded and ebonized liner of the glass. This type of "reversed" molding of the frame, ornamented with acorns and having a flat glass, has traditionally been called an Albany, New York, type because of its frequent appearance from that area. Yet recent studies have found the prototype in England.

Fire screens were defined by Thomas Sheraton as "A piece of furniture used to shelter the face or legs from the fire." Their use in Federal America was twofold: principally, to protect the facial complexions of the ladies from the scorching heat of the fireplace, and, secondly, to diffuse the annoying flicker of light from fires and candles while reading or writing at night.

There were basically two forms of floor-model screens — a pole screen and a "horse" screen. The pole form was fairly common in New York, but survivals of the "horse" screen, with a sliding frame in a trestle base, are seldom seen except in the later styles of the mid-nineteenth century. The Boscobel example (85) has a poplar frame for the pleated silk which was called "tammy" by the New York cabinetmakers. This screen fits perfectly the description of "A Horse Fire Screen" in the New York Price Books of 1796 and 1810.

The pole screen (86) at Boscobel is equally unusual in that it does not have the standard "pillar and claw" base but a flat abacus tripod base with brass paw feet in the Greco-Roman archaeological taste of George Smith's *Designs for Household Furniture* of 1808. The hinged folding screen of pleated silk has a frame of satinwood veneer over poplar, and the entire reeded pedestal and pole are of solid satinwood. This pole screen descended in the Van Rensselaer family along with the great Phyfe tea table (44) and is undoubtedly also from the Phyfe workshop.

Two American clocks in the Boscobel collection are distinguished by their elegant cases and fine brass movements. The earlier of these is the tall clock (82) by Effingham Embree, who was working in New York and was listed in the city directories from 1786 to 1794. A number of Embree's clocks in public and private collections are known by their entertaining features such as musical movements and especially moving parts in the arch of the dial. In this example, a child in a swing hanging from a tree in a cottage yard moves to and fro with the beat of the pendulum.

The case of the tall clock shows in the bell-shape of its hood, or bonnet, a New York penchant for a popular English form. It is distinguished from its prototype by an attenuated shape, which is inlaid with the ubiquitous American eagle perched, in this example, on a rosette instead of the usual globe. This peculiar and somewhat naive inlaid figure of an eagle is engraved on holly wood and is typical only of this group of New York tall clocks. The cases, of course, were not made by Embree but, as usual, by a neighboring cabinetmaker. Although none of these cases have yet been found with a label or a signature, their workmanship is analogous in style to several sideboards and desks labeled by Mills and Deming, William Whitehead and Elbert Anderson, all of whom were in business at the time Embree was selling his clocks.

The other clock in the Boscobel collection is a Willard's Patent Banjo, distinguished by the fact that it was sold by Benjamin Smith in his New York clock store and bears his name on the dial (83). The great Willard family of clockmakers in Roxbury and Boston was as famous in its day as New York's Duncan Phyfe. Their banjo clocks with eight-day brass movements were cited among the best of timekeepers and were frequently advertised for sale by New York stores. As early as November 22, 1810, an advertisement in *The Columbian* read: "Time-Pieces, Just received, and for sale by J. Tiebout, an elegant assortment of Willard's Patent Eight day Clocks." The Boscobel example is in every respect typical of the Massachusetts exports, but it is rare in retaining its original gilt and églomisé decoration, which depicts in its lower tablet a damsel with swans.

In the Dyckman estate inventory of 1806, a barrel organ is listed that was doubtless the one Dyckman had purchased in London and shipped to New York in 1803 with cases of other articles. Although Dyckman's original barrel organ has not surfaced, the one in the Boscobel collection (84) very likely resembles his own. It has a handsome mahogany case in the Hepplewhite taste, ornamented with a medallion engraving of a lady with children at a keyboard organ. Barrel organs, like pianofortes, were popular imports to New York and in some instances were being made in America. To enjoy the barrel organ, one had only to turn the crank and occasionally change the wooden cylinders. Steel pins on the cylinders picked the levers of the reeds, thus producing the different melodies; their titles were carefully inscribed on an index inside the lid. Boscobel's barrel organ is labeled by the prolific firm of musical instrument-makers Longman & Broderip, and has survived in remarkable playing condition.

Survivals in hanging lighting fixtures are extremely rare from Boscobel's period. Most of the high-style chandeliers were imported from England and France. In the collection are four

remarkable examples, the earliest of which is an "entry light" or hall lantern (88). It is similar to several illustrated by Hepplewhite in 1788, which have a vasiform, clear, blown-glass shade suspended in an ornamented, gilt-bronze frame by three chains. The pendant finial at the bottom twists out to give access to its attached candle cup.

The extraordinary carved and gilded "Mercury chandelier" (91) was found in Brighton and is believed to have been designed by William Holland about 1807. William, not to be confused with his uncle, Henry Holland, the earliest progenitor of the Regency style, was a skillful, but lesser known, designer of Neo-Classical decorations. The crown, figure, and ring are gilt-gesso or carved wood. The frieze of the

ring is ornamented with stars and Grecian anthemia, or honeysuckle, which are cast of pewter and gilded.

The classic specimen of a crystal chandelier in the French taste (90) of the early nineteenth century is probably from a Birmingham manufacturer. It has a frame of finely cast ormolu or gilt-bronze, fitted with brilliant cut-glass streamers and prismatic pendants. By 1820, the Pittsburgh glass house of Bakewell, Page & Bakewell is said to have been making crystal chandeliers. Although none seem to have survived, they must have been related in concept to this popular model of that time.

In 1783, Aimé Argand, a Swiss chemist, patented his famous oil-burning lamp. It greatly increased the intensity of the light and eliminated smoke and smell by inducing an upward draft of air through the center of a cylindrical wick mounted between two metal tubes. The oil flowed by gravity from a reservoir or font. The idea was quickly adopted by English manufacturers, who produced Sheffield and bronze Argand-type lamps. In the Boscobel collection, a striking example (89) of English Regency design incorporates the Argand principle in a hanging fixture, which must resemble in form the "patent-hanging oil lamp" listed in the 1799 inventory of Aaron Burr's Richmond Hill. A richly cut, shallow glass basin is suspended under the central font by brilliant glass streamers to catch any possible drippings of oil from above. The frame and font are cast of patinated and contrasting gilt-bronze, which is ornamented with the popular vintage motif of Bacchanalian identity.

75 Looking glass.
1800–1810, New York.
H.67 (170.2) W.22¾ (57.8)
Mahogany veneer and gilt-gesso on pine; églomisé tablet.
A paper legend on the back reads: "This glass bot by Stephen and Abigail Young, July 7, 1807, in New York. Brought on the Stage. I, Parsippany and Stephen Young went there for it—paid $18 for it." Purchase, 1976.

76

76a

76 Looking glass (pair).
1800–1810, Boston or New York.
H.62(157.5) W.42½(108.0)
Gilt-gesso on pine; églomisé tablets.
Descended in the family of Joseph
Tilden.
Purchase, 1977.

76a Detail of the other looking glass.

77 Girandole glass (mirrors, pair).
1800–1815, American or English.
H.37(94.0) W.30(76.2) to outer bobeche
Frame: Diam.21¼(54.0)
Gilt-gesso on pine; iron, wire, glass
bobeche and prisms.
Purchase, 1977.

78 Looking glass (pair, eagle and drapery).
1800–1810, English.
H.62(157.5) W.29½(74.9)
Gilt-gesso on pine.
Purchase, 1976.

77

78

79

81

80

79 Girandole glass (mirror, overmantel).
1810–1820, New York.
H.53 (134.6) W.38 (96.5)
Gilt-gesso on pine.
Purchase, 1976.

80 Chimney glass (overmantel).
1800–1810, Boston or New York.
H.65¼ (165.7) W.59½ (151.1)
Gilt-gesso on pine, églomisé tablets.
On loan from the Metropolitan Museum
of Art, 1977.

81 Pier glass.
1810–1820, American.
H.71 (180.3) W.37¾ (95.9)
Gilt-gesso and black on pine; iron chain.
On loan from the Metropolitan Museum
of Art, 1977.

82

82a

83a

83

84

84a

84b

Barrel Nº 1	Barrel Nº 2	Barrel Nº 3
1. Royal Family Minuet	1. The Myrtle Green	1. Feltons Variations
2. Minuet de la Cour	2. Gloster House	2. God Save the King
3. Nancy of the Dale	3. Hampstead Heath	3. The Lord my Pasture
4. Je suis Lindor	4. Robinson Crusoe	4. Easter Hymn
5. Senducis Rondo	5. La Bernoise	5. Evening Hymn
6. Maid of the Mill	6. Les Trois Graces	6. Burton New
7. The Rondeloy	7. La Galatea	7. Bedford
8. Death of Robin Gray	8. La Germanique	8. Angels Hymn
9. La Virginella	9. Le Allemande Favouri	9. The 100 Psalm
10. Top Sails Shiver in yᵉ Wind	10. The Swiss Allemande	10. The 104 Psalm

84 Barrel organ.
London, Longman & Broderip (working 1767–1798).
H.46¼ (117.5) W.22¼ (56.5) D.16⅜ (41.6)
Mahogany, oak, pine, holly stringing.
Purchase, 1962.

84a Label of barrel organ.

84b Barrel organ's list of melodies.

85 Horse firescreen (sliding frame).
1810–1820, New York.
H.54½ (138.4) W.19 (48.3) D.18¼ (46.4)
Mahogany, tulip poplar; pleated silk; gilt-brass reeded toe caps and rollers.
Purchase, 1976.

86 Pole screen.
1810–1820, New York, attributed to Duncan Phyfe's workshop.
H.47 (119.4) D.15½ (39.4)
Satinwood, tulip poplar; pleated silk; gilt-brass paws.
Descended in the family of Stephen Van Rensselaer, the seventh Patroon.
Purchase, 1976.

85

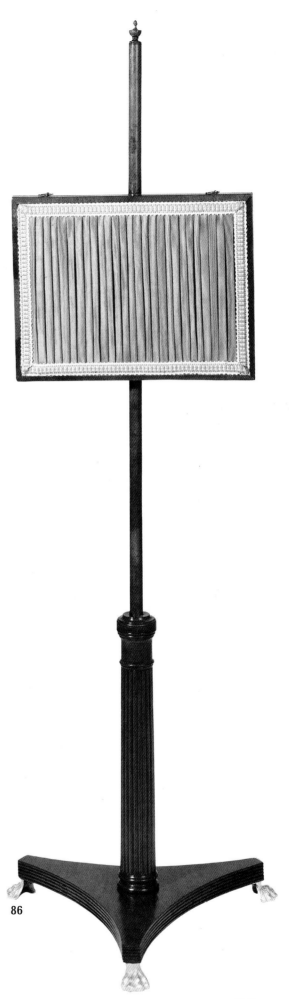

86

87

88

89

89 Patent hanging oil lamp (Argand-type).
1805–1820, English.
H.42 (106.7) Diam.22½ (57.2)
Gilt-bronze, patinated bronze; cut-glass
streamers and pendants.
Purchase, 1976.

87 Two-light Regency lusters (pair).
c. 1810, English.
H.21½ (54.6) W.15¼ (38.7)
Bronze doré and cut glass.
Purchase, 1978.

88 Hall lantern.
1790–1810, English.
H.36¼ (92.1) Diam.15¼ (38.7)
Gilt-brass and blown glass.
A similar lantern is illustrated in
Hepplewhite's *The Cabinet-Maker and
Upholsterer's Guide; or, Repository
of Design for Every Article of House-
hold Furniture* . . . (London, 1788).
Purchase, 1977.

90

90 Chandelier (French-style).
1800–1820, English.
H.42³⁄₄ (108.6) Diam.28 (71.1)
Gilt-bronze; chiseled, cut-glass streamers
and pendants.
Purchase, 1976.

91 Chandelier.
1807, London, attributed to William
Holland.
H.34½ (87.6) Diam.38½ (97.8)
Gilt-gesso on pine; iron wire and chain,
stars and anthemia of gilded pewter.
Purchase, 1976.

The Original Dyckman Possessions

The treasures in ceramics, silver, and glass that States Dyckman acquired during his last three years in London have survived in remarkable quantity and are now safely exhibited, along with other Dyckman possessions, in a special museum gallery in Boscobel. Dyckman had been anxious to prove his resources and worthiness to the skeptical family of his young wife, Elizabeth Corne. Certainly, he tried to compensate her for his long absences from home with tangible gifts both useful and beautiful. In celebration of his success in finally obtaining, in 1803, all the monies and annuities that were due him for his clerical services to a group of British Quartermasters during the Revolution, he went on a spending spree in the most fashionable shops in London. The richness of his purchases, seen here, is testimony to his expectations for a genteel life of fashionable elegance and propriety in his future mansion on his farm along the Hudson River.

By 1800, the Adamesque Neo-Classicism of Britain had pervaded the design of every object of her domestic manufacture. In ceramics, the already venerable firm of Josiah Wedgwood was the leader in pottery. Their invention, in the eighteenth century, of the exquisitely modeled jasperware had become renowned for its delicate, cameolike quality and Classical ornament. Dyckman chose the then popular dark blue-and-white shown in the surviving group (97), for which there is an original bill of sale (p. 16) from the London showrooms of Wedgwood & Byerley. Another group from a dinner service of Wedgwood's famed cream-ware (94) displays a typical "Etruscan" border of painted trompe-l'oeil Classical flutes or "lag and feather" design. Large services of such creamware were considered among the best dining equipage in America, where Chinese blue-and-white patterns on durable porcelain shapes were the common everyday wares in most households.

In the early nineteenth century, the Wedgwood potteries did not produce porcelain, but deferred to the Worcester, Derby, and Coalport factories for those who sought fashionable dishes of a vitreous body and high glaze, with elaborate gilt and painted decoration. "A Rich Dessert Service (of Coalport) painted in Landscapes to order with Gilding key and Leaf in Solid gold . . ." was purchased by Dyckman at Sharpus & Company (93). A list of the views on the plates identifies a dozen fashionable, Classical, and Romantic country seats such as Harewood, Attingham, and Fonthill. Another view on an "Ice Pail French Vase shape" shows St. Paul's Cathedral and London from the Thames River. Such fine trophies of Dyckman's British ventures were sure to delight and please the hostess and her company at Boscobel. The borders of the entire group are decorated with a Greek fret or key, the single most recurring element in the Classical vocabulary of ornament.

The silver holloware purchased by States Dyckman in London was chaste, handsome, and in the latest fashion. The shapes were purely Classical, trimmed with basic gadroon or beaded borders and panels of reeding. As early as 1788, Dyckman had shipped to New York, aboard the *Hope*, the "Plated Tea Urn" that is exhibited in the drawing room at Boscobel on the Phyfe mahogany urn stand. This Sheffield urn, bearing his cipher, is the earliest example of the Classical taste in the Boscobel collection and must have been in 1788 among the first imports of this new English shape to come to America. Likewise the Sheffield platter domes (104) and the solid silver tea set by Richard Crossley and John Emes (103), which Dyckman purchased from Walter Smith in 1803, presaged in style the successive Classical taste of the English Regency (1811–20). It is interesting to note that the pendant ring handles on the sugar bowl, made by Crossley in 1800, were adopted by the Forbes family of New York silversmiths by about 1805 and are found on similar sugar bowls made by them. At the same time, the eight fiddleback dessert spoons (106), which Dyckman purchased in London in 1803, had the newest "fiddle-shaped" handles generally not believed to be made by American silversmiths until about 1810, but remaining popular here through the 1850's.

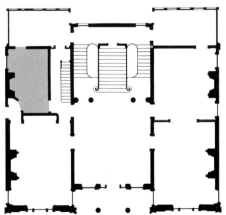

Butler's Pantry.

Other than the flatware and the tea set, the original Dyckman silver was of a fine quality of commercial Sheffield, named after the Yorkshire city in which most of the silver on copper had been produced since the discovery of the process by Thomas Boulsover in 1742.

The richest and most resplendent of all the Dyckman treasures is the pair of four-light cut-glass candelabra, at right (111), which are appropriately exhibited on the dining-room table at Boscobel. These stand over thirty-two inches high, on faceted columnar shafts of fine lead glass, supported by silver-gilt quadru-pedal bases. Dyckman purchased them in 1803 from John Blades of London, one of the most fashionable shops of the day, at a cost of forty-eight pounds. They would have been fit for any of the finest households in England and remain the single most telling clue to the domestic elegance that he planned for his new mansion on the Hudson. Elizabeth Dyck-man must have been saddened indeed when she finally placed these great candelabra in the dream-house that her ailing husband never lived to see.

92 Snuffbox.
  c. 1800, English.
  H.1¼ (3.2) L.3⅛ (7.9) W.2 (5.1)
  Gold and enamel with relief-carved
  wood portrait medallion of Charles II.
  On September 7, 1803, States Dyckman
  wrote to his wife's grandfather, Peter
  Corne: "In one of my Journeys to
  Ireland I had the good fortune to pro-
  cure a small piece of the Old Royal Oak
  which once protected a Monarch,
  out of which I had two Snuff Boxes
  made. . . ."
  On indefinite loan from Mrs. Louise
  Robinson.

93

93 Part of a "Rich Dessert Service."
English, Coalport porcelain "painted in landscapes to order."
Square compotier: H.1⅝ (4.1)
W.8⅜ (21.3)
Shell compotier: H.1¾ (4.5) W.8 (20.3)
Ice pail: H.12⅜ (31.4) Diam.7½ (19.1)
Covered sugar bowl: H.5¼ (13.3)
L.7 (17.8) W.4 (10.2)
Stand: H.1 (2.5) L.8¼ (21.0) W.6½ (16.5)
Oval compotier: H.1⅜ (3.5) L.11 (27.9)
W.7¼ (18.4)
Dessert plate: H.1 (2.5) Diam.8⅛ (20.6)
Purchased by States Dyckman from
Sharpus & Co., London, September 24,
1803.
On loan from Department of Parks, City
of New York.

94 Part of a creamware dinner service.
c. 1800, English, Wedgwood.
Large platter: H.1⅜ (3.5) L.16⅞ (42.9)
W.12¼ (31.1)
Medium platter: H.1¼ (3.2)
L.13¼ (33.7) W.9⅞ (25.1)
Small platter: H.⅞ (2.3) L.10⅜ (26.4)
W.7⅛ (18.1)
Sauce tureen: H.5 (12.7) L.8¼ (21.0)
W.6 (15.2)
"Lag and feather" border in sepia and
gold.
On loan from Department of Parks, City
of New York.

94

95 Jug (silver-mounted stoneware).
English, incised "Adams."
H.8 (20.3) W.7⅞ (20.0)
Ovoid and relief-molded with an allegorical frieze, brown glazed collar, and hinged silver cover, monogrammed "ECD."
Dyckman purchased the jug from "William Watson, Goldsmith, Jeweller and Watchmaker" in London, June 17, 1802.
On loan from Department of Parks, City of New York.

96 Part of a tea set.
c. 1800, English, Coalport porcelain.
Cream pitcher (handle repaired and reshaped): H.3⅞ (9.8) L.5¼ (13.3)
W.2½ (6.4)
Coffee cup: H.2½ (6.4) W.3½ (8.9)
Stand: H.¾ (2) L.7⅛ (18.1) W.6⅛ (15.6)
Tea pot and cover: H.5½ (14.0)
L.10⅛ (25.7) W.4½ (11.4)
Sugar bowl and cover: H.5½ (14.0)
L.5 (12.7) W.3¾ (9.5)
Saucer: H.1⅛ (2.9) Diam.5¼ (13.3)
Tea cup: H.2⅜ (6.0) W.4 (10.2)
On loan from Department of Parks, City of New York.

95

96

130

97 Part of a service of "Deep blue and white Jasper cameo."
English, Wedgwood.
Saucer: H.1 (2.5) Diam.5⅛ (13.0)
Tea cup: H.1⅞ (4.8) W.3¼ (8.3)
Tea pot and cover: H.5⅛ (13.0)
W.8¼ (21.0)
"Flower Pot": H.6 (15.2) Diam.4¾ (12.1)
Saucer: H.⅝ (1.5) Diam.4¾ (12.1)
Coffee cup: H.2¾ (7.0) W.3½ (8.9)
Purchased by States Dyckman from
Wedgwood & Byerley, London, August
29, 1803.

97

98 Cut-glass sweetmeat dish (one of four).
c. 1800, English or Irish.
H.1½ (3.8) L.5 (12.7) W.3⅜ (8.6)
Probably purchased by States Dyckman
from John Blades in 1803.
Gift of Mr. and Mrs. Fred D. Thompson.

99 Classical cut-glass covered punch bowl
and stand.
c. 1820.
Punch bowl and cover: H.11 (27.9)
Diam.10¼ (26.0)
Stand: H.1⅞ (4.8) Diam.12 (30.5)
Cut in a design of swags and strawberry
diamonds.
According to family tradition, the set
was received as a wedding gift by Peter
Corne Dyckman and his bride, Susan
Matilda Whetton, in 1821 or 1822.
Gift of Mr. and Mrs. Fred D. Thompson.

99

98

100

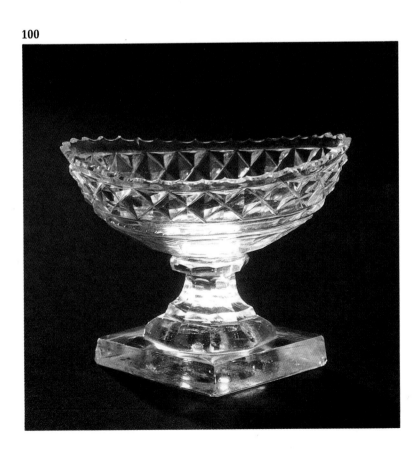

101

100 Cut-glass salt dish (one of a pair).
   c. 1800, English or Irish.
   H.3⅜ (8.6) L.4 (10.2) W.2½ (6.4)
   Probably purchased from John Blades
   in 1803.
   Gift of Mr. and Mrs. Fred D. Thompson.

101 Pair of George III cut-glass tea caddies
   with silver tops, contained in an inlaid
   satinwood box.
   Late eighteenth century, English.
   Box: H.5⅞ (14.9) L.7⅛ (18.1)
   W.5⅜ (13.7)
   Caddies: H.4⅞ (12.4) L.4⅛ (10.5)
   W.2¾ (7.0)
   Silver tops are monogrammed "SMD."
   Purchased by Dyckman from John
   Folgham, London, September 6, 1786.
   On loan from Department of Parks,
   City of New York.

102 George III traveling liquor set.
   c. 1800, English.
   Case: H.11 (27.9) L.15¼ (38.7)
   W.10⅝ (27.0)
   Consists of 6 quadrangular decanters,
   6 small decanters, 2 wine glasses, and a
   mixing bowl, contained in original
   wooden case, hinged, cornered, and
   studded in wrought iron and showing
   remnants of original paper lining.
   On loan from Department of Parks,
   City of New York.

102

103 Tea service, silver.
English.
Tea pot, sugar basin, and milk pot by
Richard Crossley, London, 1800.
Matching coffee pot by John Emes,
London, 1803.
Tea pot: H.9¼ (23.5) W.9¼ (23.5)
Milk pot: H.4⅛ (10.5) W.5½ (14.0)
Coffee pot: H.5⅞ (14.9) W.10⅝ (27.0)
Sugar basin: H.4⅛ (10.5) W.6⅞ (17.5)
All pieces bear the monogram "ECD."
Gift of Mr. and Mrs. Fred D. Thompson.

103

104

105

104 Dome-shaped covers for platters.
c. 1800, Sheffield, England, silver plate.
Large dome: H.10 (25.4) L.18⅞ (47.9)
W.14 (35.6)
Medium dome: H.9¼ (23.5)
L.16¾ (42.6) W.12½ (31.8)
Small dome: H.7¾ (19.7) L.13 (33.0)
W.10⅛ (25.7)
Monogrammed "ECD." Purchased by
States Dyckman from Walter Smith,
London, November 28, 1803.
On loan from Department of Parks,
City of New York.

105 Silver fish server, ladle, serving fork
and spoon.
Fish server, serving fork and spoon
monogrammed "ECD" and made by Eley
& Fearn, London, c. 1803. Shipped on
board the *Commerce*, September 30,
1803.
Fish server: L.10⅞ (27.6) W.2¾ (7.0)
Ladle: L.13⅜ (34.0) W.3¼ (8.3)
Serving fork: L.10⅞ (27.6) W.2 (5.1)
Serving spoon: L.10⅞ (27.6) W.2⅛ (5.4)
Ladle bears "SMD" cipher. Made by
William Simmon, London, 1784–1785,
and purchased by Dyckman from John
Folgham & Son, London, in 1788.
Gifts of Mr. and Mrs. Fred D. Thompson.

106 George III silver dessert spoon
(one of six).
1803, London, made by Richard Cook
and monogrammed "ECD."
L.7 (17.8) W.1½ (3.8)
Purchased from Walter Smith,
September 28, 1803; shipped on board
the *Commerce*, September 30, 1803.

106a George III silver salt spoon.
1802–1803, London, made by William
Eley & William Fearn, monogrammed
"ECD."
L.4⅞ (12.4) W.1 (2.5)

106b George III silver ladle (one of two).
1803, London, made by William Eley &
William Fearn.
L.7 (17.8) W.2⅜ (6.0)
Monogrammed "ECD." Purchased from
Walter Smith, London, September 28,
1803. Shipped on board the *Commerce*,
September 30, 1803.
Gift of Mr. and Mrs. Fred D. Thompson.

107 Pair of George III hot-water dishes.
c. 1800, Sheffield, England, silver plate
with wood handles and feet.
H.8 (20.3) L.14⅛ (35.9) W.8 (20.3)
Monogrammed "ECD." Purchased by
States Dyckman from Walter Smith,
London, November 28, 1803.
On loan from Department of Parks,
City of New York.

106   106a   106b

107

108

108 George I silver tankard.
1719, London, made by George Sanders.
H.7⅜ (18.7) W.7⅛ (18.1)
Presented to Elizabeth Dyckman's
great-grandfather in 1720. Inscribed,
"The Gift of Mr. Jn° Thornton and
Mr. Wm Wilberforce merchants of Hull
and Mr. Robert Thornton Merchant
in Lond^n to Mr. Peter Corne 1720."
Purchase, 1978.

108a Detail of tankard.

109 Meat platter.
c. 1800, Sheffield, England, silver plate.
H.2⅝ (6.7) L.22⅜ (56.8) W.16½ (41.9)
Monogrammed "ECD." Purchased by
States Dyckman from Walter Smith,
London, November 28, 1803.
On loan from Department of Parks,
City of New York.

108a

109

110 Silver candle snuffer and Sheffield plate tray.
c. 1800, English, "SMD" cipher.
Snuffer: H.1⅛ (2.9) L.6⅛ (15.6)
W.2⅜ (6.0)
Tray: H.⅞ (2.3) L.10 (25.4) W.3⅞ (9.8)

110a Pair of silver-plate mugs (with glass bottoms).
c. 1800, Sheffield, England.
H.5⅞ (14.9) W.6 (15.2)
Monogrammed "ECD." "2 plated Quart Muggs" were among the goods that Dyckman shipped to New York on board the *Commerce*, September 30, 1803.

110b Pair of silver-plate bottle coasters (with turned wood bottoms).
Late eighteenth century, Sheffield, England.
H.1½ (3.8) Diam.5¼ (13.3)
Shipped on board the *Montgomery* in 1788 or 1789.
On loan from Department of Parks, City of New York.

110

110a

110b

111 One of a pair of Classical 4-light
candelabra.
c. 1800, English.
H.32⅝ (82.9) W.11½ (29.2)
Vermeil and cut glass.
"1 Pair 4 light Candelabras, Cut, gilt &
ornamented . . . £48" was purchased
by States Dyckman from John Blades,
London, September 28, 1803.
On loan from Department of Parks,
City of New York.

111

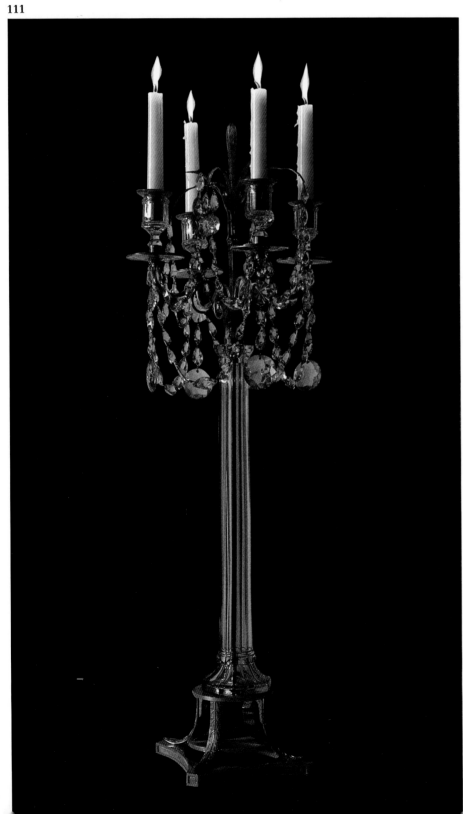

112

112 George III hot-water urn.
Late eighteenth century, Sheffield,
England, silver plate.
H.21 (53.3) W.10¾ (27.3)
Engraved with a bow knot and garland
and monogrammed "SMD."
Dyckman shipped a "Plated Tea Urn"
on board the *Hope* in 1788.
On loan from Department of Parks,
City of New York.

The Painting Collection

The Dyckman papers include numerous lists, receipts, and catalogues of States Morris Dyckman's possessions, collected here and abroad as amenities to eye, mind, and spirit.

In the 1806 estate inventory, there are twenty listings of no less than seventy-seven "pictures." From the descriptions and prices of thirty-five of these, it appears likely that at least this number were paintings. Eight, by inference or statement, were oil paintings on canvas. Twenty-seven others in a similar price range (from $2.50 to $10.00) seem to have been oil paintings as well; one of this number, a ship "in Ivory," was probably a miniature.

Of the seventeen paintings in the Boscobel collection today, six are of Dyckmans and their relations by marriage. With the exception of two religious pictures listed in the inventory as "1 Picture of Jesus Christ" and "1 ditto finding of Moses" (each valued at $5.00), paintings that have been purchased in recent years either fulfill the descriptions in the Loyalist's estate or admirably represent contemporaries or events relating to him and to his family.

113

The oldest portraits in the collection are the most interesting. The paintings of Elizabeth Dyckman's great-grandparents and some of their children have recently been attributed to John Watson, Scottish emigré to Perth Amboy in the early eighteenth century, on the basis of an entry in the artist's 1726 account book recording paintings for Dr. Henderson in New York City.

Mrs. Dyckman's grandfather, Peter Corne, is seen in a miniature by an unidentified artist. Three more unknowns recorded the visages of States, Elizabeth, and their son, Peter Corne Dyckman. Likenesses of a New England ship's captain and his wife, contemporaries of States Dyckman, recall his many trips to England and return on vessels similar to those owned by Joseph Tilden of Boston.

Ammi Phillips' portraits of Tobias Teller and his wife are of other contemporaries: Tobias Teller's immediate ancestors were Westchester County neighbors of the Dyckmans. As patriots—in contrast to Dyckman's Royalist sympathies—the Tellers underline the complex relations that existed in New York during the Revolution.

Narcissus by Benjamin West is an especially apt selection for

Boscobel. West, Pennsylvania-born, was Dyckman's contemporary in England, where he had become court painter to George III, and friend and instructor to a host of American artists who visited England before and after the Revolution.

Two large eighteenth-century Italian landscapes, an English marine view, and two later Hudson River landscapes aid in bringing together the complex web of States Dyckman's life and many interests.

Mary Black
Curator of Paintings, Sculpture, and Decorative Arts
The New-York Historical Society

113 *Peter Corne* (1722–1807), by an unidentified artist.
Miniature: oil on ivory, c. 1805.
H.2¾ (7.0) W.2¼ (5.7)
Painted near the end of his life, this miniature of Peter Corne in his early 70s is by an unidentified artist. Corne was born in Hull, England, but by 1751 was located in New York, where he married Elizabeth Henderson, daughter of Dr. and Mrs. James Henderson. Peter Corne's daughter, Letitia (1755–?), was Elizabeth Dyckman's mother.

The painting descended in the family through Elizabeth Dyckman's aunt Elizabeth Corne who, in 1783, married Baron Charles August de Girancourt de Vourecourt, Lt. of Artillery and Deputy Quartermaster General of Hessian Troops in New York in the Revolution, an indication of Loyalist sympathies in both the Dyckman and Corne families.

114 *Peter Corne Dyckman* (1797–1824), by an unidentified artist.
Oil on canvas, c. 1805.
H.26½ (67.3) W.21½ (54.6)
Peter Corne Dyckman, named for a maternal great-grandfather, was the only son and the surviving child of Elizabeth Corne and States Dyckman. He lived for only one year after his mother's death in 1823. He married Susan Matilda Whetton, by whom he had one child, Eliza, who later married Col. John Peach Cruger. The costume and hair style seen in the portrait suggest a date of about 1805. Peter Corne Dyckman was eight years old that year.

115 *States Morris Dyckman* (1755–1806), by an unidentified artist.
Oil on canvas, c. 1785.
H.23⅝ (60.0) W.19½ (49.5)
The costume that States Dyckman wears dates to the mid-1780's. The sophisticated style of the handsome portrait suggests that it was painted when Dyckman was in England between 1782 and 1788, working for the British Quartermaster Generals.

Dyckman died in 1806 and was buried in the Dyckman Family Burial Ground at the north end of Manhattan Island. His gravestone describes one appraisal of his complex personality: "His manner was polite, his taste refined, his conjugal love was pure, his parental strong. His hospitality sprang from benevolence, his charity from feeling and a sense of duty. Highly esteemed in life he was sincerely lamented in death." In 1909, the graves of States Dyckman, his wife, and two children were removed to Cedar Hill Cemetery of the Dutch Reform Church of Cortland Town, Montrose, New York, near the original location of Boscobel.

116 *Elizabeth Corne Dyckman* (1776–1823),
by an unidentified artist.
Oil on canvas, c. 1800.
H.33 (83.8) W.26 (66.0)
On loan from Department of Parks,
City of New York.
Like her husband, Elizabeth Corne was
the descendant of a distinguished
New York family. Her parents and
grandparents were Peekskill residents.
At eighteen, she married States Dyck-
man, twenty-one years her senior.

The costume in this portrait dates to
about 1800. In May of that year, Dyckman sailed for England for the first
time since their marriage on Feb. 1, 1794.
He was to remain there for three and
a half years. Two months after his
departure, their second child, Letitia
Catalina Dyckman, died in infancy.

It was Elizabeth Corne Dyckman
who, after her husband's death, continued his plans for Boscobel, oversaw
the construction of the house, and
supervised the installation of the extensive furnishings and library listed in
the inventory of her husband's estate.

117 *Tessie (Thysie, Thysje) Benson Henderson (b. 1699) and Children,* attributed to John Watson (1685–1768).
Oil on canvas, 1726.
H.54 (137.2) W.41 (104.1)

118 *Dr. James Henderson* (d. 1743) *and Daughters*, attributed to John Watson (1685–1768).
Oil on canvas, 1726.
H.54 (137.2) W.41 (104.1)

The imposing and colorful portraits of Dr. and Mrs. James Henderson and their children are attributed to John Watson of Perth Amboy, New Jersey. Watson, like Henderson a Scotsman, was not only an artist but a landowner, merchant, and businessman in New Jersey and New York.

Dr. and Mrs. Henderson were the great-grandparents of Elizabeth Corne Dyckman. Henderson owned several large parcels of land in Manhattan and held royal patents to extensive acreage in the New York Province. He was a physician and merchant in New York. It is likely that it was through their similar interests that Henderson and Watson became acquainted and that the portraits were commissioned.

In Watson's 1726 account book, he mentions painting three "picktors" for Dr. Henderson. The children in the man's portrait have been restored from two shadow images that appear to have been covered over by the original artist soon after they were painted. This is borne out by the appearance of the same children in Mrs. Henderson's portrait.

119 *Tobias Teller* (1772–1854), by Ammi
Phillips (1788–1865).
Oil on canvas, c. 1817.
H.29⅝ (75.3) W.23½ (59.7)

120 *Caroline (or Paulina) Sammis Teller,*
by Ammi Phillips (1788–1865).
Oil on canvas, c. 1817.
H.29⅝ (75.3) W.23½ (59.7)
Tobias Teller's grandfather, William
Teller, settled along the Hudson on land
purchased from the Indians, immedi-
ately south of the original location of
Boscobel. Known as Teller's or Croton
Point, the site figured in several inci-
dents in the Revolution, the most
important relating to the patriot skir-
mish against the English warship
Vulture, anchored off Teller's Point.
Because of the action, Major André
missed his intended rendezvous with the
Vulture, after his meeting with Benedict
Arnold, and was forced to make
his fatal journey to New York by land.

The Tellers were related to the
Dyckmans through marriages with
members of the Vermilyea family. These
subjects were residents of Red Hook
in Dutchess County. Their portraits date
to about 1817, when Ammi Phillips lived
and worked in that area.

121 *Sarah Parker Tilden* (1761–1827),
attributed to Ralph Earl (1751–1801).
Oil on canvas. c. 1785.
H.33½ (85.1) W.26¼ (66.7)

122 *Joseph Tilden* (1753–1800), attributed to Ralph Earl (1751–1801).
Oil on canvas. c. 1785.
H.33½ (85.1) W.26¼ (66.7)
Boston shipowner and ship's captain Joseph Tilden married Sarah Parker of Brookline late in 1777, during the Revolution in which he served the American cause. The paintings are attributed to the Loyalist Ralph Earl, who had fled the colonies, barely escaping hanging in 1778. In England, Earl gravitated to the studio of the American painter Benjamin West. Returning to America through the port of Boston in 1785, Earl is believed to have painted the Tilden portraits in the late spring of that year.

123 *Narcissus,* by Benjamin West (1738–1820).
Oil on canvas, 1808.
H.23½ (59.7) W.36 (91.4)
Several Greek myths were delineated by Benjamin West, Cupid and Psyche being his most frequent legendary subjects. But the tale of the beautiful youth Narcissus, infatuated by his own reflection, was the subject of one of his most highly praised paintings on a mythical theme.

Created by West in 1808, *Narcissus* remained in his "splendid and unequalled Exhibition Rooms" in Newman at Oxford Street, London. After the artist's death in 1820, attempts were made to aid his family by selling the works that remained in his New Gallery.

Narcissus was described in almost the most extravagant terms of any of the paintings in the sale, held in May, 1829: "No work of the hand of West excited more general admiration among the professors of the art, than this very original and finely conceived cabinet picture. That recondite quality in painting, so well expressed by Sir Joshua Reynolds, in the term *"low toned brightness"* is herein displayed with rare felicity. . . . The contemplation of this small picture, ever open to the view of the student, afforded new light to the rising school of landscape painters, and quickened those perceptions, which have raised it to the decided pre-eminence which it has attained, as acknowledged by all the world."

124 *Scenery in the Catskills*, by Thomas Doughty (1793–1856).
Oil on canvas, c. 1830 or 1839–40.
H.35⅜ (89.9) W.26⅝ (67.6)
Thomas Doughty was one of the earliest painters of the Hudson River School. His first commission as an artist was completed in 1821. After studying at the Pennsylvania Academy of Fine Arts, Doughty continued his career in Philadelphia and Boston, with side trips to New Hampshire, Maine, and New York. Two years in England added to his renown as a landscape artist. Upon his return to America, Doughty spent some time in Newburgh, New York, and it is to this period that *Scenery in the Catskills* is assigned.

125 *View of West Point* by an unidentified
artist in the style of Thomas Chambers
(1808–after 1866).
Oil on canvas, c. 1850's.
H.31½ (34.3) W.41¾ (106.1)
Its date set at mid-nineteenth century by
the presence of the side wheeler
Thomas Powell in the foreground, this
painting of West Point is in the tradition
of numerous views of the military
academy, based on engravings after
works by Hudson River School painters

such as Thomas Doughty and William
H. Bartlett. Among these copyists,
Thomas Chambers is best known,
although this painting appears to be in
a less accomplished style than his.

126 *Marine View*, by an unidentified artist.
Oil on canvas, c. 1785.
H.23⅝ (60.0) W.35⅜ (89.9)
On loan from Department of Parks,
City of New York.
Typical of late eighteenth-century
marine painting, this attractive view of
a sailing ship is the kind of scene
with which States Dyckman would have
been familiar. He himself made three
trips to and from the British Isles on
vessels similar to this.

127 *Italian View*, inscribed "A.S.F. Ging?
1795."
Oil on canvas, 1795.
H.33 (83.8) W.44¼ (112.4)

128 *Italian View*, by an unidentified artist.
Oil on canvas, c. 1790–1800.
H.33⅛ (84.1) W.41½ (105.4)
It has been suggested that these views,
by two different artists, are by followers

of the Italian Adrien Manglard. They
date to a period in which States Dyckman was spending much of his time
in Great Britain. In this period, English
collectors looked to Italian painting
as the ideal; these views, derivative of
High Renaissance style, are typical
of the works that Dyckman and his contemporaries sought for their collections.

Acknowledgments

No recital of acknowledgments would be complete without a further expression of our gratitude to Lila Acheson Wallace. Her contributions have been extolled elsewhere in this volume, but it bears repeating that without her assistance, the research, reevaluation, and refurbishment of Boscobel could never have been accomplished. Mrs. Wallace's only request was that Boscobel remain a place of beauty, a stipulation we were delighted to observe.

The initial *Critique and Proposals for the Historic Furnishings of Boscobel*, prepared by Berry B. Tracy, Curator-in-Charge of Decorative Arts, the American Wing of the Metropolitan Museum of Art, mapped out our course of action, and his advice and guidance throughout the project were invaluable. We are especially indebted to him for his erudite treatment of the furniture collection in this volume.

Mary Allis, long a Director of Boscobel, encouraged us in the early stages of our work and she applied her extensive knowledge of the homelier details of early American life to the refurbishing of Boscobel's kitchen.

We are grateful to Florence Montgomery for her guidance in the selection of appropriate textiles, and to Richard C. Nylander, Curator of Collections for the Society for the Preservation of New England Antiquities, for making available to us the resources of the Society's unique collection of document wallpapers. His colleague Morgan Phillips, Architectural Conservator for the Society, analyzed paint samples and advised us in the reproduction of original colors.

Historic research is the backbone of any restoration project. Boscobel appreciates the continued interest of Julia A. Thompson, who began her study of States Dyckman in the 1950's. Our staff member Barbara W. Bielenberg spent countless hours gleaning valuable information from microfilms of the Dyckman papers at The New-York Historical Society, and she wishes especially to thank the Society's library staff and particularly Thomas J. Dunnings, Curator of Manuscripts, and his assistant, William Asadorian, for their patient assistance.

Mary Black, Curator of Paintings, Sculpture, and Decorative Arts for The New-York Historical Society, merits our warm appreciation for contributing to this volume her expert analysis of Boscobel's painting collection. Her attribution of the Henderson portraits is a major breakthrough in the study of the Hudson Valley limners.

Many gifted and knowledgeable people helped bring about the renaissance of Boscobel in two memorable but hectic years. Edward V. Jones, architect and special consultant to the White House, used his knowledge of Federal period architecture to solve some troublesome design problems. Harold and Robert Sack of Israel Sack, Inc., not only helped us find furnishings of impeccable quality, but also supervised the restoration of a number of pieces that had lost their original luster and brilliance.

We are grateful to Mrs. Murray Douglas, of Brunschwig & Fils, Inc., who reproduced for us period wallpapers from the collection of the Society for the Preservation of New England Antiquities and documents in the Brunschwig collection.

Others who deserve mention are Albert Wadsworth of Hugh McKay Ltd., carpet mills of Durham, England; Henrietta Blau of Delta Upholstery; Scalamandre Silks, Inc.; and the talented Peter Guertler, who painted the interiors and executed the patent floor cloth to Ed Jones' specifications.

Lastly, our very special thanks to our able staff members Gwendolyn Heuston and Jeanne Shupe, who not only handled endless phone calls, purchase orders, and invoices, but, on more than one occasion, cheerfully provided our consultants with delicious lunches on very short notice!

Credits

The prints and documents on pages 12, 16, 17, and 19 appear courtesy of Boscobel Restoration. The watercolor *Workshop, Showroom, and Warehouse of Duncan Phyfe* by John Reuben Smith, Rogers Fund (22.28.1) as well as the print on page 25 appear courtesy of the Metropolitan Museum of Art. All photographs of the interiors, architectural views, and the original Dyckman possessions are by Frank Moscati. The print on page 14 appears courtesy of the New-York Historical Society, and those on pages 13, 15, and 18 courtesy of the New York Public Library, Astor, Lenox and Tilden Foundations. All photographs of the furniture and paintings in the collection are by Taylor and Dull. The book was designed by George Klauber and Joseph Roberts, George Klauber Inc., and produced by Harry N. Abrams, Inc.

Notes

1 States Morris Dyckman left behind more than 1,300 letters, bills, and other items of business and personal correspondence. Microfilms of these papers are lodged at the New-York Historical Society, 170 Central Park West, New York, New York 10024. Unless otherwise noted, the information contained in this essay is based on the Dyckman microfilms.

2 In 1651, King Charles II of England, defeated by the forces of Oliver Cromwell at the Battle of Worcester, fled to safety in France. For forty-three days he traveled, disguised as a peasant. The third day of his wandering was spent hiding in the limbs of a great oak in the Forest of Boscobel, about twenty-six miles from Worcester in the County of Salop.

3 Four of States Dyckman's brothers served the American side in Capt. James Kronckheit's company of the Westchester County Militia (Grenville C. Mackenzie, *Families of the Colonial Town of Philipsburgh,* courtesy Sleepy Hollow Restorations, Tarrytown, New York, 1976). States' brother Benjamin rose to Lieutenant *(Documents Relating to the Colonial History of the State of New York,* ed. Berthold Fernow, Albany, 1887, Vol. XV, p. 306). The activity of States' oldest brother, Sampson, as a messenger for the Committee on Conspiracies is documented in the *Journals of the Provincial Congress, Provincial Convention, Committee of Safety of the State of New York, 1775–1777,* Albany, 1842. A letter from George Clinton, Governor of New York, to General George Washington, September 27, 1780, indicates that Sampson was also involved in intelligence activities for the Americans (Clinton Papers, New-York Historical Society).

4 The Dyckman microfilms document these purchases. See also *Records of Westchester County Clerk's Office,* White Plains, New York: Liber N, pp. 489-94; Liber 39,

pp. 454-56; *Book of Mortgages,* Liber G, p. 62.

5 William Strickland, *Journal of a Tour in the United States of America, 1794–1795,* ed. Rev. J. E. Strickland (New-York Historical Society, New York, 1971) p. 93.

6 *Abstracts of Wills,* Volume III, 1730–1744 (New-York Historical Society, New York, 1894) p. 416. *Calendar of New York Colonial Manuscripts Indorsed Land Papers in the Office of the Secretary of State of New York, 1642–1803* (Albany, 1864). Volumes VIII, IX, XII, and XIII list numerous petitions and patents for lands in Orange and Ulster Counties and the Mohawk Valley in Henderson's name. The Mohawk grant is recorded in *Book 12 of Patents* (Office of the Secretary of State, Albany, New York) p. 57.

7 Letter of Jacobus Swartwout, Joseph Strang, and Melancton Smith to Commissioners of Sequestration in Westchester County, March 20, 1777, in *Old New York Reminiscences,* Dr. John W. Francis (New York, 1865), Vol. XIII, #127, New-York Historical Society. Letter from Peter Corne to General Alexander McDougall, April 9, 1777 (McDougall Papers, New-York Historical Society).

8 A "long soffa (sic)," a set of ten chairs with "2 pair of arms," a pair of card tables, and a bedstead were ordered from Gifford & Scotland, September 11, 1793; an ingrain carpet, "6 full trim'd window curtings (sic)" and other trimmings from P. Norwood in September and November 1793; and a pair of looking glasses from William Wilmerding, November 1793. These and other bills for carpentry and painting survive.

9 States Dyckman's "benefits" exceeded a half-million of today's dollars, according to a formula advanced by Charles Montgomery in *American Furniture, The Federal Period* (New York, 1966). Montgomery suggested that 1810 prices,

quoted in New York dollars, be multiplied by ten or twelve to arrive at comparable figures today. Allowing for inflation since 1966, the figure for the Dyckman "benefits" would be considerably more than $500,000.

10 File No. 8-1807, States M. Dyckman, Westchester County Surrogate's Office, White Plains, New York.

11 *Ibid.*

12 Agreement between Henry I. Cruger and Susan Matilda, his wife, and Eliza Letitia Corne Cruger, January 2, 1838. Liber 77, p. 147. Westchester County Clerk's Office, White Plains, New York.

13 Obituary, John Peach Cruger, *New York Times,* August 31, 1888.

14 The Grantor files of the Westchester County Clerk's Office, White Plains, New York, contain a number of Cruger leases. The indenture between John P. Cruger & wife and William H. Carrigan, December 12, 1848 (Liber 134, p. 70), is typical: providing for the use of sheds, machines, dwelling house, and barn, the privilege of taking sand, clay, and fresh water for making bricks, and allowing for pasturage for horses, cows, and oxen.

15 As early as 1857, Eliza Letitia Corne Cruger and her husband, John Peach Cruger, had mortgaged Boscobel to George and William Douglas, the sons of Margaret Corne Douglas, aunt of Elizabeth Dyckman and creditor of her husband, States (Liber 235, pp. 163-68, Westchester County Clerk's Office, White Plains, New York). A foreclosure sale resulted in the transfer of title to Boscobel to William P. Douglas, George Douglas' son, on May 14, 1880 (records of the Westchester County Clerk's Office, Liber 980, pp. 259–61). In 1885, William P. Douglas sold the property to Herbert C. Plass and wife, of New York City (Liber 1061, p. 21). The Crugers must have remained in Boscobel after this date, for John Peach Cruger's 1888 *New York*

Times obituary states that he died "at the old manor house, Boscobel."

16 The private files of Boscobel, Inc., and Boscobel Restoration, Inc., document the organizations' efforts to save Boscobel. The struggle also received extensive press coverage. See especially: Charles Messer Stow, *Boscobel to Be Razed March 1 If No Plan to Save It Appears, New York Sun,* January 2, 1942; *VA Completes $5,000 Boscobel Mansion Job, Evening Star,* Peekskill, New York, April 11, 1952; Denslow M. Dade, *Hudson Settlers' Relic Is Saved, But in Pieces, New York Herald Tribune,* February 26, 1956; Merrill Folsom, *Hudson River Mansion Lives Again, New York Times,* May 21, 1961.

Selected Bibliography

HISTORY OF BOSCOBEL

Abstracts of Wills, Volume III, 1730–1744. New York, New-York Historical Society, 1894.

Calendar of New York Colonial Manuscripts Indorsed Land Papers in the Office of the Secretary of State of New York, 1642–1803. Albany, 1864.

Fernow, B., ed. *Documents Relating to the Colonial History of the State of New York.* Albany, 1887.

Journals of the Provincial Congress, Provincial Convention, Committee of Safety of the State of New York, 1775–1777. Albany, 1842.

MacKenzie, G. *Families of the Colonial Town of Philipsburgh.* Tarrytown, N.Y., Sleepy Hollow Restorations, 1976.

Montgomery, C. *American Furniture of the Federal Period 1788–1825.* New York, 1966.

Strickland, W. *Journal of a Tour in the United States of America 1794–1795.* New York, New-York Historical Society, 1971.

THE COLLECTION

Ackermann, Rudolph, ed. *The Repository of Arts, Literature, Commerce, Manufacture, Fash-ions, and Politics.* London, 1809–28.

Bailey, Chris N. *Two Hundred Years of American Clocks and Watches.* Englewood Cliffs, N.J., 1975.

Bonaparte, Joseph Napoleon. *Catalogue of Rare, Original Paintings . . . Also of Valuable Engravings, Elegant Sculpture, Household Furniture, &c. &c., Belonging to the Estate of the late Joseph Napoleon Bonaparte . . . to be sold at his late residence, near Bordentown . . . Friday, June 25, 1847 . . .* Copy of catalogue in the American Wing Archives, Metropolitan Museum of Art, New York.

Cornu, Paul, ed. *Meubles et Objets de Goût 1796–1830, 678 Documents Tirés des Journaux de Modes et de la "Collection" de La Mésangère.* Paris (n.d.).

Hope, Thomas. *Household Furniture and Interior Decoration, Executed from Designs by Thomas Hope.* London, 1807.

Huger, Sarah. Letter to Mrs. Daniel Horry, Tradd Street, Charleston, South Carolina (New York, January 4, 1816). Copy in the American Wing Archives, Metropolitan Museum of Art, New York.

Ingerman, Elizabeth A. "Personal Experiences of an Old New York Cabinetmaker." *Antiques,* Vol. 84, No. 5 (November 1963), pp. 576–80.

Johnson, William. "A Young Man's Journal of 1800–1813 (William Johnson of Newton, N.J.)." *New Jersey Historical Society, Proceedings,* n.s., Vol. 8 (1923), as quoted in Bayrd Still, *Mirror for Gotham: New York as Seen by Contemporaries from Dutch Days to the Present.* New York, 1956.

The Journeymen Cabinet & Chair Makers' New-York Book of Prices. New York, 1796.

Lea, Zilla Rider, ed. *The Ornamented Chair, Its Development in America.* Rutland, Vt., 1960.

Longworth, David, ed. *American Almanack. New-York Register, and City Directory for the Thirtieth Year of American Inde-pendence.* New York, 1805–6.

McClelland, Nancy. *Duncan Phyfe and the English Regency 1795–1830.* New York, 1939.

Metropolitan Museum of Art. *A Loan Exhibition of New York State Furniture.* New York, 1934.

Metropolitan Museum of Art. *Nineteenth-Century America: Furniture and Other Decorative Arts.* New York, 1970.

Miller, Edgar G., Jr. *American Antique Furniture,* 2 vols. New York, 1937.

Museum of the City of New York. *Furniture by New York Cabinetmakers 1650 to 1850.* New York, 1956.

The New-York Book of Prices for Cabinet & Chair Work agreed upon by the Employers. New York, 1802.

The New York Book of Prices for Manufacturing Cabinet and Chair Work. New York, 1817.

The New-York Revised Prices for Manufacturing Cabinet and Chair Work. New York, 1810.

Otto, Celia Jackson. *American Furniture of the Nineteenth Century.* New York, 1965.

Palmer, Brooks. *The Book of American Clocks.* New York, 1950.

Rice, Norman S. *New York Furniture Before 1840 in the Collection of the Albany Institute of History and Art.* Albany, 1962.

Shearer, Thomas, et al. *The Cabinet-Makers' London Book of Prices, and Designs of Cabinet Work, calculated for the convenience of cabinet makers in general. . . .* London, 1788.

Sheraton, Thomas. *The Cabinet-Maker and Upholsterer's Drawing-Book in Three Parts . . .* Vol. 1, pts. 1, 2, London, 1793; Vol. 2, pt. 3, London, 1794; 3rd ed., rev. and enl., in 4 pts., London, 1802.

Smith, George. *A Collection of Designs for Household Furniture and Interior Decoration. . . .* London, 1808.

Tracy, Berry B. "For One of the Most Genteel Residences in the City." *The Metropolitan Museum of Art Bulletin,* n.s., Vol. 25, No. 8 (April 1967), pp. 283–91.

Tracy, Berry B., and William H. Gerdts. *Classical America 1815–1845.* Newark, Newark Museum, 1963.

THE PAINTING COLLECTION

Abstracts of Wills, Volume III, 1730–1744. New York, New-York Historical Society, 1894.

De Sola Pool, D. *Portraits Etched in Stone, Early Jewish Settlers 1682–1831.* New York, 1952.

Doughty, H. N. *Life and Works of Thomas Doughty.* Typescript. New York, New-York Historical Society, 1941.

Dunlap, W. *The History of the Rise and Progress of the Arts of Design in the United States.* New York, 1834; repr. 1969.

Goodrich, L. B. *Ralph Earl, Recorder for an Era.* Albany, 1967.

Groce, G. C. and D. H. Wallace. *The New-York Historical Society's Dictionary of Artists in America.* New Haven, Conn., 1966.

Haacker, F. C., comp. *Burials in the Dyckman-Nagel Burial Ground.* New York, 1954.

Hastings, Mrs. R. "A John Watson Discovery." *Antiques,* Vol. 96 (1939), pp. 26–27.

Huntting, I. *History of Little Nine Partners.* Amenia, N.Y. 1897.

Linzee, J. W. *The History of Peter Parker and Sarah Ruggles of Roxbury, Mass., and Their Ancestors and Descendants.* Boston, 1913.

Lossing, B. J. "The First Painter in America." *American Historical Record* (Philadelphia), Vol. 1 (1872), pp. 337–38, 456–66.

Morgan, J. H. "John Watson, Painter, Merchant and Capitalist of New Jersey, 1685–1768." *American Antiquarian Society, Proceedings* (Worcester, Mass.), October 1940, pp. 1–101.

————. "Further Notes on John Watson." *American Antiquarian Society, Proceedings* (Worcester, Mass.), April 1942, pp. 1–12.

Riker, J. *Revised History of Harlem.* New York, 1904.

Robin, G. *A Catalogue Raisonné of the Unequalled Collection of Historical Pictures, the Works of the Revered and Highly Gifted Painter, the Late Benjamin West, Esq.* London, 1829.

Rybolt, M., comp. *Stoutenborough History.* Typescript. Kenney, Ill., 1968.

Sawitsky, W. *Ralph Earl 1751–1801.* New York, Whitney Museum of American Art, 1945.

Sniffen, H. S. and A. C. Brown. *James and John Bard, Painters of Steamboat Portraits.* Newport News, Va., 1949.

Watson, J. "The Account and Copy Book of John Watson, 1701–1740's with Additions by Alexander Watson." Manuscript. New York, New-York Historical Society.

Index

Entries in roman type refer to page numbers; entries in *italic type* refer to numbered illustrations. Other illustrations are indicated by "illus." and their page numbers.